The
MAXIMUM
ENERGY

COOKBOOK
AND
NATURAL FOOD
PREPARATION
MANUAL

BY SHARON BROER

The Maximum Energy Cookbook by Sharon Broer
Published by B & A Publications
100 Ariana Blvd
Auburndale, Florida 33823

Library of Congress Catalog Card Number:
ISBN 0-9716215-1-9

This book is not intended to provide medical advice or to take the place of medical advice and treatment from your personal physician. Readers are advised to consult their own doctors or other qualified health professional regarding the treatment of their medical problems. Neither the publisher nor the author takes any responsibility for any possible consequences from any treatment, action or application of medicine, supplement, herb or preparation to any person reading or following the information in this book. If readers are taking prescription medications, they should consult with their physicians and not take themselves off medicines to start supplementation without the proper supervision of a physician.

Printed in the United States of America

ACKNOWLEDGEMENTS

I wish to express my love and
appreciation for my husband, Ted, for his
patience and love through the year of
preparing this cookbook. I thank him also
for taste-testing every recipe, together
with several others that did not pass the test.

To my happy, healthy children, Austin, Harrison,
Alexis and Savannah. God has shown me,
by raising them to be healthy eaters,
that it's true, "we are what we eat."

To my mom, Shirley Bennett,
my thanks for patiently and tirelessly
proofreading my cookbook.

DEDICATION

This cookbook is dedicated to all of
the wonderful people we have had the privilege
to help and inform.

TABLE OF CONTENTS

INTRODUCTION

As a nation, we simply must change the way we eat. Today more individuals are suffering from degenerative diseases than ever before. The average American diet consists of fast foods and processed ingredients that deny the body adequate nutrition.

Over the last twenty years I have formed strong convictions about nutrition and diet, and I've committed my life to helping others to live healthier.

The recipes you will find in this cookbook will take you "back to the nutritional basics" of fresh, wholesome food. I have created tasty, satisfying dishes that your entire family will enjoy by using fresh fruits, vegetables, and grains. It is my prayer that you will enjoy preparing these recipes as much as I have enjoyed making them.

When my husband, Ted, and I were first married, I assumed that I was walking in perfect health because I didn't have a major disease such as cancer or heart disease. As Ted and I began working together as a team in the field of nutrition, I quickly discovered how little I actually understood regarding healthy eating. What I had considered as perfect health was actually far from it.

Many of us assume that we are healthy, even if we have any of the following symptoms of ill health:

Indigestion	Stress
Heartburn	Menstrual Problems
Allergies	Headaches
Depression	Sinus Trouble
Irritability	Constipation
Nervousness	Fatigue

How about you? Are you in good health? One look in your medicine cabinet can be extremely revealing. If you are like most of us, your medicine cabinet contains one or more of the following items that signal poor health:

Antacids	Sedatives
Pain killers	Anti-cough medicine
Decongestant	Tranquilizers
Aspirin	Anti-depressants

Americans as a whole rush through their days feeling less healthy and alive than we should. We must take a closer, more honest look at the state of our health. Why do we often feel tired, edgy and just plain unwell? Too often we treat the symptoms of our ill health, but never address the causes. Do people have headaches because they have an aspirin deficiency? Or, do people take Rolaids because they have an antacid deficiency? No! But, we often turn to such medications to remedy the results of nutritional deprivation and imbalance.

In my own life, I had not realized that the miserable headaches I constantly suffered were caused by my body's elevated blood sugar levels. I battled these headaches daily, usually refusing to take pain relievers. With constant pain between my temples in the front of my head, often the last thing I felt like doing was being nice to people. Being often irritable did not help me to create a peaceful home environment. Can you relate?

You see, I was addicted to sugar. You may ask "How can an individual be addicted to sugar?". VERY EASILY! My worst weakness was for mint chocolate chip ice cream — I could eat two huge bowls at one sitting. When grocery shopping, my shopping cart would feel drawn to the ice cream freezer by an invisible magnet! Once I even wondered if the grocery store had developed special carts as a marketing tool. However, after checking another cart I realized the magnet was not in the cart — it was in me!

I have never had to seriously watch my weight. Many of our friends and clients tell me that I am blessed. But in my case it was no blessing. I stayed so hyped-up on sugar that my body burned calories as fast as I ingested them. When I learned that my body was aging more quickly than normal because of these high sugar levels, I decided to make some drastic changes. I began listening intently to all of the nutritional advice that my husband, a leading nutritionist, could give me.

I eliminated all sugars from my diet. White sugar can act as a drug upon the body. If you are having any sugar problems, such as symptoms of hypoglycemia or diabetes, it's best to eliminate all sugars, including fructose, honey and all refined and processed foods. All of the above cause an immediate rise of the sugar levels in the body. Instead of iced tea, I began drinking steam-distilled water only, at least eight to ten glasses a day.

It took two years to get my body's sugar level perfectly balanced. You see, it had taken twenty-six years for it to get into that condition. Two years didn't feel like that much time. Today I can enjoy dessert now and then without getting a headache. But here's a word of caution: In most cases, it's not what you eat between Christmas and New Year's Day that hurts you; it's what you eat between New Year's Day and Christmas that damages your body. In other words, it's not the little occasional treats we enjoy, but it's the nutritional lifestyle we live day by day that determines that course of our health.

Discovering the health and vitality that a lifestyle of good nutrition can give has changed my life completely. Healthy eating can change your life as well. I have attempted to compile the practical insights and wisdom that I have learned through the years as I have attempted to raise a family to eat and live healthier. These tasty, healthy, recipes, tips for feeding children, shopping tips, and helpful information for the holidays and much more will be a valuable tool for you to learn to achieve maximum energy and walk in health all the days of your life.

I thank God for bringing Ted and me together and for allowing us to spread this message of health and vitality to all of you. It is my sincere prayer that this cookbook and food preparation manual will help you and your family to make the dietary changes necessary to live a healthier, more abundant life!

Simplifying
the Supermarket
Safari

1

Simplifying the
Supermarket Safari

Where does your family's healthier nutritional lifestyle begin? With developing new grocery store shopping habits, of course. But, let's face it, grocery shopping is easy to dread...fighting traffic, hauling sacks, long lines, bumping into carts and having other carts ram into yours... the list goes on.

When you add the importance of reading labels on today's products, it becomes even more frustrating. Steel up your courage, square your shoulders and let's get started. The benefits of a healthy lifestyle will be well worth the initial investment. First, you must learn to speak the language...label language, that is.

Learning to Speak the Label Language

It is wise to understand the language of labels. Of course it would be easier to simply believe that manufacturers are only concerned about your family's health and would never add anything to your food products that could harm you. I don't.

As consumers, we must make it our responsibility to become educated on this subject. A food label is a contract between the consumer and the manufacturer. Like many contracts, labels may be difficult to understand, and what is omitted may be as important as what is included.

First, understand what has been added to the food you are feeding your precious family, and why. There are two main groups of additives: direct and indirect additives.

1. Direct additives

These additives include flavorings, preservatives, buffers, neutralizers, stabilizers, texturizers, emulsifiers, colorings, bleaches and sanitizing agents.

Here are several facts you should know:

Fact 1. Finding the ingredients on a label can sometimes be as difficult as reading or pronouncing them. They may be hidden under flaps or folds, and sometimes they are printed with such fine print that you need a magnifying glass to see them.

Fact 2. Don't be misled when a product states "All Natural Ingredients," or "No Preservatives Added," or even, "Natural Fruit Flavors, with real fruit Juice." This does not mean the product contains no harmful additives. The Manufacturer uses such wording to make you, the consumer, feel better about the product.

Fact 3. Ingredients are listed on the label according to quantity used. The ingredients used in the largest quantity will be listed first, and the ingredients used in the smallest quantity will be listed last.

Fact 4. Here's a good rule of thumb: The longer the list of ingredients, the more likely the product contains chemical additives.

Fact 5. Even food purchased at a whole food market or a health food store can contain harmful additives. Always read the label!

Fact 6. Organic foods should contain indirect additives. They may be a little more expensive, but are worth the money.

Fact 7. There are more than three thousand indirect and direct common food additives in our diet, nearly two-thirds of them are flavorings used to replace the natural flavors lost during processing.

Fact 8. The majority of food additives have nothing to do with the nutritional value of our food.

Fact 9. As of 1972, thirty-five widely used additives were approved for human consumption, but have since been removed as unsafe. Most of them were found to cause cancer. In 1978, food additives were a 1.3 billion-a-year business. Today, it is a more than 4.5 billion-dollar enterprise.

Fact 10. It is a sad fact, but when nothing is added to foods, they cost us considerably more. For some examples:
- Unbleached flour costs 4 times more than bleached.
- Unsulfured raisins cost 6 times more than those that are treated.
- Untreated tomatoes cost 5 times more than regular canned tomatoes.

2. Indirect Additives

Included in this group are additives from packaging, processing, pesticides and animal drugs[a1]. Although you don't find these additives mentioned on product labels, it's important to understand that the foods we purchase nevertheless contain these substances. Food labels ought to reflect this fact!

Here are some interesting facts of which you may be unaware:

- Tranquilizing drugs are injected into many pigs immediately before transport to slaughter, making a withdrawal period impossible, thus giving diners unexpected sedation with their pork dishes?

- Sixty percent of all herbicides, ninety percent of all fungicides and thirty percent of all insecticides are carcinogens? (Carcinogens are substances that can cause cancer).

- Pesticides are one type of indirect food additive of concern, but another involves residues from animal drugs. The Food and Drug Administration has been trying to rein in the use of antibiotics in animal feed since 1972. Nevertheless, cattle and poultry continue to be fed antibiotics to increase their growth. Antibiotic-resistant infections in humans are on the rise, and scientists world-wide are blaming animal husbandry practices as an important cause.3

- Consumers and scientists have been fighting for two decades to stop the use of hormones used to increase the growth of cattle, swine and poultry. Despite their efforts, these powerful drugs are still widely employed. The female hormone estrogen is added directly to the food supply, and may be creating adverse effects. In addition, Environmental Protection Agency announced in October of 1993 the emerging evidence indicating that the insecticide endosulfan, as well as other chemicals that imitate estrogen, may be associated with instance of breast cancer.

The Most Common Additives to Avoid

A person would have to become a chemist to keep up with all the chemicals and poisons added to our foods.

To simplify the process of reading labels, I have taken the most common additives that I come across during my weekly grocery shopping trips. If more than two additives are listed on a label, then I do not even waste my time reading the label. If I find any of the following additives in the food I plan to purchase, I return that item to the shelf and search for another brand.

Exitotoxins

MSG-(monosodium glutamate) or also known as "Chinese-restaurant syndrome."

- It is used to intensify meat and spice flavoring.
- It has a salty taste.
- Reported complaints are headache, chest pains, numbness, irritability and depression.
- Baby food processors are mandated to remove this from baby food.
- May cause permanent brain and nerve damage.
- MSG is also listed under other names such as hydrolyzed vegetable protein (HVP) or "natural flavoring."

Aspartame (Nutrasweet/Equal)

Aspartame (Nutrasweet/Equal) is composed of the following:

- **Methanol** — a neurological poison that cannot be made non-poisonous. It causes headaches, blindness and permanent brain damage.
- **Aspartic Acid** — an excitotoxin, similar to MSG. It has been known to over-stimulate the neural cells causing cell death. This is why it is called an excitotoxin because it literally kills brain cells. Studies done by Dr. John Olney, at Washington University School of Medicine in St. Louis, Missouri, have shown that it creates holes in the brains of animals that were tested.7
- **Phenalaline** — causes permanent brain damage if concentrations are high enough.

When aspartame is ingested, these three components are released, which can cause side effects. Dr. Olney has shown when aspartame is combined with nitrites (found in hot dogs, luncheon meat, bacon, and sausage,) a compound known as diketopiperazine can be formed, further chemically degrading to a nitrosourea. Nitrosoureas can produce malignant brain tumors in experimental animals. That means that if you combine a pepperoni pizza with a diet soda or bacon and eggs with coffee sweetened with Nutrasweet, additional cancer causing substances may be created by the combination. These simple combinations may be the answer to the huge increase in malignant brain tumors in both adults and children in this country. Several years ago when this problem came to national attention, cell-phones were blamed. But there has also been a corresponding increase in children getting brain cancer as well, however children do not use cell-phones. Personally, I believe that aspartame is the culprit fueling this surge of brain cancer.

Hydrogenated or partially hydrogenated oil

This process turns liquid oil into a solid. Hydrogenated oil adversely affects the level of fat in the blood and has been linked to colon cancer. It is found in margarine products and Crisco-type products, and it is the very cheap oil used in chips, crackers, cereal, peanut butter, snack cakes, some breads, and many, many more products. Avoid cottonseed oil, palm kernal oil and corn oil as well. I recommend using virgin cold press olive oil for regular use or use raw certified butter.

Nitrites

Nitrites are used to give that pretty pink color to cured meats, bacon, bologna, hot dogs, ham, Vienna sausages and luncheon meats.

- Nitrites combined with natural stomach acids create nitrosamines, which are powerful cancer-causing agents.
- Baby food manufacturers voluntarily removed nitrates from baby foods in the early seventies.
- In 1977, Germany banned nitrites and nitrates except for use with certain species of fish.

Olestra or Olean (fake fats)

Olestra or Olean (fake fats) were introduced to the American consumer market in 1996. They are a combination of soybean oil and sucrose that has been manipulated into molecules too large to be absorbed or digested by the human body. In preliminary studies, it was found Olestra caused tumors in laboratory animals. Possible side effects include intestinal cramping and loose stools. In short, if you buy a product containing Olestra, make sure you purchase some Pampers at the same time.

Mono and Diglycerides

These are synthetically made from emulsifying and defoaming agents.

- They are used in bakery products to maintain softness.
- They are also used in beverages, ice creams, shortening, margarine, chocolate, whipped toppings and cosmetic creams.
- Mono and diglycerides are on the Food and Drug Administration's list of food additives to be studied for possible effects upon human reproduction.

BHA (Butylated Hydroxyanisole)

This is the preservative used in many products, including beverages, ice cream, baked goods, potato chips and breakfast cereals.

- In November, 1990, Glenn Scott, M.D., filed a petition with the Food and Drug Administration asking the agency to prohibit the use of BHA in food. [footnote: Winters, Ruth, M.S. A Consumer's Dictionary of Food Additives, Three Rivers Press, N.Y.; 1978, p. 94]

BHT (Butylated Hydroxytoluene)

This is a preservative used in the same types of products as BHA.

- Experiments at Michigan State University found that BHA appeared to be less toxic to the kidneys than BHT.
- Some consumers have complained of allergic reactions.
- "The possibility that BHT may convert other ingested substances into toxic or cancer-causing agents should be investigated," according to the Select Committee of the America for Experimental Biology, which advises the FDA on food additives. [footnote: ibid. p.95]
- BHT is prohibited as a food additive in England.

Aluminum

- Aluminum is frequently used in food additives, cosmetics and deodorants.
- Ingestion of this substance can aggravate kidney and lung disorders.
- Aluminum deposits have been found in the brains of Alzheimers' patients.

Aluminum Sulfate

Aluminum Sulfate is used in producing sweet and dill pickles.

- It is also used as an antiseptic, astringent and detergent in deodorants.
- This substance is moderately toxic by ingestion and injection.
- Aluminum may affect reproduction.

Artificial Flavorings

More than 2,000 flavorings are added to foods, with approximately 500 being natural and the remainder being synthetic.

This is by far the largest category of additives:

- Natural lemon — benzaldehyde (synthetic)
- Natural orange — methylsalicylate (synthetic)

Artificial Food Colorings (F, D and C colors)

Artificial food colorings include any dye, pigment or other substance capable of coloring food, drugs, or cosmetics. Artificial colors offer considerable health risks, with absolutely no known health or nutritional benefits.

- In 1900 — more than eighty dyes were used to color food. The same dye could be used to color clothes as could be used to color candy.
- In 1938 — Colors were given numbers instead of chemical names. Fifteen food colors were used at this time.

- In 1950 — Children were made ill by coloring used in candy and popcorn. Since these incidents, orange (numbers 1 and 2); red, (numbers 1 and 32); yellow, (numbers 1,2,3 and 4); and violet (number 1) have been banned.

- In 1976 — Red, (number 2) was removed because it was found to cause tumors in rats. Red, (number 4), which was used for coloring Maraschino cherries, was also banned due to cancer causing agents.

In 1996, my husband Ted, our son Austin, and I attended a wedding reception. We saw friends we had not see for years. Our son was nine years old at the time. He and some friends were "checking out" the food. The punch table was separate and off in a far corner. The punch consisted of some type of bright, thick red liquid. My husband came over to me and asked how much punch Austin had drunk. I hadn't been paying much attention, so he confronted Austin. Austin admitted to drinking four glasses. I went over to the punch bowl and thought to myself "Oh no, red dye!" Later that night when we got home, Austin's voice became very raspy. In the next three to four days he was constantly blowing his nose. He literally had a cough for four months. His young body had never been exposed to artificial colorings like that, and for him these were high excessive levels.

I have emphasized the preservatives and colorings we ingest, but what about all the ones we put on our skin? Our skin is very porous and whatever we apply to our skin, is quickly absorbed. As an experiment, try rubbing a cut clove of garlic on the bottom of your foot to see how quickly it is absorbed. Within thirty minutes you will taste it in your mouth.

Knowing this, I was still shocked when a doctor friend of ours told my husband and me a true story about one of her patients. The doctor was running some chemical tests on this patient, trying to find out what was causing some of her problems. When the test results came back, the doctor found unusual high levels of blue dye #1. The patient was totally puzzled because she was so careful to read labels and avoid artificial colorings. After much thought and several questions about the products she had put on her skin, the patient admitted to the doctor, "You know, I have been washing my dishes everyday for the last twenty five years in blue dish washing liquid." There was the answer to the "blue" mystery.

Whatever you do, make sure you consider reading labels and giving up your favorite brands as a benefit. A little extra time, care, and consideration can extend your life and the lives of those you love. Your good health is worth the effort!

Grab a Grocery Cart!

Now I am going grocery shopping with you. We will have a great time, and I trust that as you practice this several times, healthy grocery shopping will become much easier and quicker. The kids will love helping you identify the "no, nos". I will be taking you down each aisle (of my local store the way it is arranged). Your grocery store may be set up differently, but the overall grouping of foods are the same.

Where to Shop?

My first choices: whole food markets. Health food stores have come a long way since the 1960's and 1970's. In larger population areas, we are now seeing whole food markets and natural food stores replacing the health food stores.

1. Whole food markets offer organic vegetables, bakeries and delicatessens and a large selection of natural foods and personal care items.

2. Local organic produce markets. These markets offer a great selection of organic and locally grown produce. Many grocery stores now include entire sections of health foods.

3. My third choice is shopping at the cleanest grocery store available. Why? The cleanest stores are usually the busiest, which indicates they will carry the freshest produce. Many grocery stores are beginning to carry complete selections of organically grown produce and health food sections.

Why Organic?

One western Massachusetts vegetable grower discovered after fifteen years of chemical farming that his land was literally "dead soil". His soil looked nothing like it did when he began farming. Not even an earthworm could be found in the hard-rock soil. He realized that if there was any hope for reviving his farmland he would have to begin using organic farming techniques. Today, the former chemical-dependent farmer is now a successful organic food producer with fertile and productive soil.

Certified organically grown produce has to be grown in soil that is pesticide free for three years. Then the soil is worked back to a natural state.

Organically grown fruits and vegetables are free of the many chemical additives and pesticides that we discussed. According to polls a large majority of American consumers would choose organically grown over chemically grown food if the prices were compatible.

I do realize that the higher cost of organically grown produce is the deciding factor that discourages many consumers. I used to feel the same way, but the more I learned about chemicals and additives in our food, the more I decided to get creative at shopping and spending. What I mean by creative spending is comparing the differences between what I would have spent on high-priced junk food and what I spend on organic foods. The savings more than compensates for my organic food purchases. In addition, I am investing in foods that are beneficial to my family's health, just not appealing to our stomachs.

Organic food production is on the increase. Farmers are realizing the importance of keeping soil alive and productive, thus making the demand for foods grown without toxic chemicals increasingly popular.

Our Shopping Itinerary

Let's travel together up and down the grocery store aisles and select the healthiest brands. Grab a cart, and let's go shopping!

The Dairy Aisle

Milk Choices:
- First: Raw Certified goat's milk
- Second: Raw Certified milk
- Third: Non-fat dry milk
- Fourth: Low fat milk

Milk purchased in the local grocery store usually comes from cows loaded with hormones, antibiotics and steroids. We as health conscious consumers should be concerned about the new bovine growth hormone being administered to dairy cows. *The International Journal of Health Services* in the January, 1996, issue, released a study concluding that consuming milk from cows treated with BGH increased one's risk of breast and colon cancer. [Footnote: "EPA Study on Insecticide for Links to Cancer," New York Times, Oct. 24, 1993, p.21.]

Raw certified milk is hard to find. The non-fat organic brand I use from Walnut Acres is convenient since you can make up a quart at a time whenever needed. The raw milk and non-fat dry milk are also not homogenized. Milk should be used in moderation, in recipes or over oatmeal or cereal. A calcium supplement can always be taken to ensure an adequate amount of calcium.

Buttermilk Choices:

- First: Organic
- Second: Grocery Store

I only use buttermilk in a few recipes, but we do not purchase it just to drink it as a beverage.

Butter Choices:

- First: Raw certified organic
- Second: Organic
- Third: Grocery store brand without dyes

My favorite brand is *Organic Valley*. Always buy butter with the lightest color, which usually means no artificial colors have been added. I always purchase the lightly salted variety for better flavor. Butter is better for you than margarine. Margarine is a trans fat (trans-fatty acid) or hydrogenated oil. These trans fats, according to Harvard School of Public Health, contribute to 30,000 deaths from coronary artery disease each year in the U.S. [[M.W. Gillman, et. al., "Margarine Intake Subsequent Coronary Heart Disease in Men," Epidemiology, 1997 Mar; 8 (2): 144-149.]]

Cheese Choices:

- First: Raw certified organic
- Second: Organic
- Third: Cheese with only milk cultures and salt without dyes

My favorite brand is *Organic Valley*. You should avoid processed cheeses that contain emulsifiers, lactic acid, colorings, and preservatives. Avoid cheese slices. Choose cheeses in small block rectangles that are very light in color.

Cottage Cheese Choice:

- Organic low fat

My favorite brand is Organic Valley. You should make sure your cottage cheese contains live culture, lactobacillus, bulgaricus and streptococcus thermophilus. These live cultures are very valuable for those taking antibiotics. They help replenish important intestinal bacteria destroyed by antibiotics.

Yogurt Choices:

- First: Raw or organic goat milk yogurt
- Second: Raw or organic sweetened with fruit juice

My favorite brand is *Stoneyfield* and *Redwood Hill Farm*. Your yogurt choice should contain live cultures like the cottage cheese. These cultures aid digestion and even help to make milk more digestible for lactose intolerant consumers.

Egg Choices:

- First: Organic natural
- Second: Grocery store natural eggs — antibiotic free

Be sure you avoid eggs containing hormones, steroids and antibiotics. Some people may be blessed to have neighbors or friends who have their own laying hens that actually peck the ground and eat bugs. If you purchase from someone who has hens, be sure to offer them a fair price.

Canned Goods Aisle

I use very few canned goods from the grocery store, and then only in an emergency. But I didn't say I did not use canned goods. I use organic canned goods that have special coated can interiors preventing lead seams touching the food.

Canned Soup:

- First: Health Valley, Walnut Acres

Canned Fruit:

- If I need crushed pineapple, I buy the whole pineapple and crush it myself.

Canned Beans:

- First: Eden brand

Canned Salmon:

- Chicken of the Sea

Mexican and Italian Food Choices

Canned Bean Dip:

- First: Bearito Organic

Taco Sauce or Picante:

- First: Any organic brand in grocery store that does not have preservatives or   additives.

Pasta Sauce:

- First: Milina Organic
- In the grocery store, a good brand is Classic all natural.

Pasta:

- Stores are now offering fresh pasta. You should try to buy that kind.

Condiment Aisle

Mayonnaise Choice:
- A brand without canola oil
- I do not buy mayonnaise in the grocery store.

Catsup Choices:
- Haines with a pop up lid or Westbrae
- I do not buy catsup in the grocery store.

Mustard Choice:
- Any natural brand

Tamari Sauce Choice:
- Any natural brand
- Tamari sauce is like Soy sauce.

Worcestershire Sauce Choices:
- A health food store brand

Peanut Butter Choices:
- Fresh ground or any other brands that contain only peanuts and salt.

Jelly Choices:
- Any organic brand
- Any grocery store brand that contains only fruit, very little sugar, and no additives.

Baking Goods Aisle

Flour Choice:
- Arrowhead Mills

Baking Powder Choice:
- Any non-aluminum brand

Spices Choice:
- Frontier brand or any non-irridated brand

Sweetener Choices:

- Stevia
- Scannt
- Fructose
- date sugar
- honey
- natural maple syrup

Biscuit Mix Choice:

- Arrowhead Mills

Cookie Mix / Brownie Choice:

- Simple Organics
- Maury's cookie dough
- Tom's cookie dough

Cake Mix Choice:

- Simple Organics

Coffee, Tea, Cereal Aisle

Coffee Substitute Choices:

Any of the following:

- Roma Capuccinio
- Roma
- Sipp

Just yesterday I received information on a new product; Organic Decaf, which uses natural water process.

Tea Choices:

- Organic Green Tea

Cereal Aisle

High Fiber Choices:

- First: Good Friends by Kashi (8 grams of fiber)

- Second: Grainfield Raisin Brand (7 grams of fiber)
- Third: Arrowhead Mills Bite Size Shredded Wheat (6 grams of fiber)

Look for the highest in fiber. Brands should not have hydrogenated oils nor any other additives.

Oatmeal Choice:

- Arrowhead Mills, old fashioned (not instant)

Grits Choice:

- Arrowhead Mills (white or yellow)

Meat Counter:

Chicken Choices:

- First: Sheldon Free-Range
- Second: Purdue also claims to raise hormone free chickens.

Beef Choices:

- First: Farm raised, local, leanest possible or organic

Hot Dog Choice:

- Kosher Hot dogs with no nitrites
- Salmon dogs

I have never been able to find hot dogs that do not contain nitrites in a grocery store. Whole food markets carry some brands, but they are high in fat.

Frozen and Prepared Frozen Food

Fruit and Veggie Choice:

- Cascadian Organic

Meatballs:

- Sheldon

Pot Pies and Apple Pies:

- Amy's

Bread, Crackers, Cookies, Chips

Bread:

- First: Ezekial bread
- Second: Sprouted grain bread
- Third: Any whole grain bread that does not contain hydrogenated oils, mono-or diglycerides BHT or BHA, or other preservatives. Check your whole food market bakery.

Crackers:

- First: Ritz look a likes by Tree of Life
- Second: Saltines by Barbara
- Third: Any whole grain cracker that does not contain hydrogenated oil, mono-glycerides or diglycerides or other preservatives.

Chips:

- First: Corn chips by Bearito
- Potato chips by Barbara
- Second: Popcorn — microwave Bearitos brand (does not contain hydrogenated oils)

Try several types of the above items and find your favorite. We do not keep these in the house all the time, but just have on special occasions. We look for brands not using hydrogenated oils or canola oil.

Food Descriptions

Have you ever picked up a package in the health food section and wondered what it was, and for what use? Join the club. It is one more dimension of learning the language of healthy eating. The following descriptions of healthy foods, what they are called, and the reasons for using them, may really help.

Grains

Brown Rice — is unprocessed, organically grown rice with the bran layer still intact.

Bulgur — Cracked wheat. Bulgar wheat is great for hot cereal and makes a good replacement for meat in chili and soups.

Corn grits — is coarsely grown corn. Corn grits make a good breakfast or side dish for dinner. We prefer white grits. We add cheese.

Millet — is probably the most misunderstood and undervalued grain. Known to some as "bird seed", millet makes a good cereal and replacement for rice.

Rolled Oats — are the unprocessed, non-instant oats, and are rich in iron and calcium.

Whole grains — include barley, buckwheat, rye and wheat. These grains mix well with rice and make very nutritious cereals.

Flour

Barley flour — is ground from organically grown barley grain, and it makes a great hot baby cereal.

Brown Rice Flour — is ground from organically grown brown rice, and it makes great cookie batter mixed with whole-wheat flour.

Buckwheat Flour — is ground from organically grown buckwheat, and it makes excellent pancakes.

Cornmeal — is ground from organically grown corn, and it is higher in mineral content than any of the other flours. Fresh ground cornmeal makes "melt-in-your-mouth" cornbread.

Rye Flour — is ground from organically grown whole grain rye. Here's a great mixture flour: one pound of barley, one pound of rye, and one pound of wheat.

Soy Flour — is ground from soybeans and mixes well with whole-wheat flour.

Whole Wheat Flour — is ground from organically grown hard, red winter wheat, and it combines well with other flours.

Whole Wheat Pastry Flour — is ground from soft spring wheat. Excellent for making cookies and pastries.

Unbleached Wheat Flour — can be used to make fluffier cakes.

Artichoke Pasta — is pasta made from American Jerusalem artichoke flour. It makes non-starch pasta with great flavor.

Tortillas

Corn — is from whole grain corn with no preservatives or additives.

Whole Wheat — is from whole wheat flour. No lard or preservatives are used.

Sweeteners

Barley Malt Syrup — is a very mild sweetener made from barley grain.

Black Strap Molasses — is not very sweet, but it is very high in trace minerals and iron. I use it in moderation because of its very strong flavor. This is not traditionally used as a sweetener, but when you do, it provides an added benefit of supplementing your family's diet with iron.

Brown Rice Syrup — is a very mild sweetener made from brown rice and barley. Brown rice syrup is my favorite sweetener.

Fructose — is the sugar found in fruit. Use it as a substitute for white sugar.

Maple Syrup — is the boiled down sap from maple trees. I use Shady Maple Farms brand. Also, Sam's Club sells a good natural 100% maple syrup at a low price.

Sorghum — is a mild tasting molasses which is also high in trace minerals. I use this in place of honey.

Tupelo Honey — is raw, unpasteurized and unfiltered. This type of honey is used by diabetics more often than any other honey.

Dried Fruit — is an excellent natural sweetener. Make sure it is not dipped in honey, and has no sulfur added.

Unsweetened coconut — provides great flavor, and it is rich in calcium.

Date Sugar — is sugar from dates.

Stevia — natural herbal sweetener.

Condiments

Agar Agar — Can be used in place of gelatin.

Natural Catsup — Has no sugar, preservatives or artificial coloring added.

Natural Mustard — Contains no additives.

Baking Soda — Use low sodium brands.

Baking Powder — Use aluminum free varieties.

Mayonnaise — Choose natural, with no canola oil.

Seasonings and Flavorings

Carob Powder — is a great replacement for chocolate. It is sweeter than chocolate without caffeine.

Cayenne Pepper — is red in color and is much hotter than black pepper.

Garlic Powder — is a quick seasoning when you don't have the time to sauté garlic.

Nacho Seasoning — I use Frontier Herbs brand in Mexican dishes and on bread or popcorn.

Barley Miso — is made from naturally aged organic grains and beans. Barley miso is high in enzymes and great for seasoning foods.

Kelp — is a sea vegetable with a natural salty flavor.

Popcorn Seasoning — Frontier Herbs brand.

Tamari — is similar to soy sauce.

Wow! That was a quick trip! I sincerely hope our shopping excursion has helped you decide which types and brands are healthy and which ones you need to avoid. Grocery shopping will become increasingly easier as you learn the language and continue in your commitment to healthy living.

NOTES

Bountiful
Breakfast

Fruit and Whole Grains
Breakfast Treats
Helpful Hints for Cooking Grains

2

Bountiful Breakfast

If you have school children, you've probably noticed them too: the pudgy little school children who trudge off to the bus stop early in the morning, carrying a donut in one hand and a can of soda pop in the other. It's no wonder an epidemic of obesity is sweeping the children of our nation, not to mention hyperactivity, diabetes, cancer, and Attention Deficit Disorder!

If you are serious about your commitment to your family's health, breakfast is priority one. Children, as well as adults, need to start the day with a healthy nutritious breakfast. I call breakfast our family's "fuel meal". A healthy breakfast should consist of "live foods" that fuel the body for the remainder of the day. As a parent it may be impossible to control what your child eats for lunch, which makes it even more important that they receive a high fiber, nutritious breakfast.

The average American breakfast usually consists of sugary boxed cereal, processed orange juice, and/or processed breakfast bars. This breakfast is ideal for someone seeking a high sugar-low fiber diet. Did you know that some boxed cereals contain as much as 68 percent sugar? Sugar robs the body of vital nutrients. High fat, low nutrition breakfasts can cause your children to be overfed and undernourished.

Make a new commitment right now to begin your days with a healthy fruit or natural whole grain "fuel meal". We start the day with a protein shake — even our children enjoy them. (Our 14 year old has been drinking them since he was 2!)

Candy for Breakfast?

Just how much sugar is in popular sugary breakfast cereals? Far too much! The following list of the sugar content in many cereals may shock you. Some popular children's cereals actually contain more than fifty-percent sugar. Varieties of candy contain less! As you read through the following list, ask yourself if it's any wonder that so many youngsters struggle to pay attention at school. Educate your children to the importance of eating wholesome food for breakfast! It will benefit them enormously throughout their lives.

Listed below are some favorite children's breakfast foods and approximate percentage of refined carbohydrates.

Sugar Content:

All Bran 20%
Bran Buds. 30.2%
Cap'n Crunch 43.3%
Cocoa Krispies. 45.9%
Cocoa Pebbles 53.5%
Fruit Loops 47.5%
Frosted Flakes. 44%
King Vitamin 58.5%
Life 14.5%
Lucky Charms 50.4%
Pink Panther 49.2%
Sir Grapefellow 40.7%
Sugar Smacks 61.3%
Super Orange Crisp. 68%
Trix 46.6%
Chocolate Chip Breakfast Bar 31.8%
Chocolate Malt Instant Breakfast 40.4%
Vanilla Breakfast Bars 40.4%

Fruit for Breakfast

Fruit is a highly concentrated carbohydrate, which makes it an ideal fuel with which to start the day. Fruit is also very easily digested. Because of its high fiber content, fruit is an excellent roughage food, and it is loaded with vitamins.

Eat fruit early during the day since the natural sugar it contains provides energy. We have our fruit every morning in our protein shake.

Here's a tip: Variety is the key. Be creative, experiment, and learn to love the fresh flavor of fruit at the start of each day. In addition, try substituting some of the following fruits with other similar ones in the various fruit recipes in this chapter. [a6] I highly recommend any of the following as wonderfully delicious breakfast fruits:

Apple	Loquat
Apricot	Mango
Avocado	Nectarine
Banana	Orange
Blackberries	Papaya
Blueberries	Paw Paw
Boysenberries	Peach
Cantaloupe	Pear
Casaba melon cherries	Persimmon
Cranberries	Pineapple
Currants	Plum
Dates	Pomegranate
Figs	Prickly Pear
Gooseberries	Prunes
Grapefruit	Quince
Grapes	Raisins
Guava	Rhubarb
Honeydew melon	Raspberries
Kiwi	Strawberries
Kumquat	Tangerine
Lemon	Starfruit
Lime	Watermelon

Grains in Boxed Cereals
vs.
Natural Whole Grains

Have you ever taken a minute to compare the processed grains found in most breakfast cereals with more natural whole grains? Let's take a closer look:

Open a box of your favorite cereal. What's inside?

I'm not sure, but I think I see wheat, barley, oats, rice or corn. It's hard to tell since the grains are processed, refined and stripped of fiber. Then they are smashed, rolled, flattened, and/or puffed. The best value may be the toy surprise inside the box!

Natural Whole Grains

Nothing compares to the nutritional value of whole grains. The benefits to your body are endless, and they are delicious tasting too!

Here is a list of several natural whole grains. Which ones have you never tried? When preparing interesting breakfast grains for your family, variety is the spice of life!

Amaranth	Millet
Barley	Rolled Oats
Buckwheat	Steel-cut oats
Bulgur	

How to Cook Grains

	Water	Cooking Time	Yield
1 cup Barley	3 cups	1¼ hour	3½ cups
1 cup Buckwheat	2 cups	20 minutes	2½ cups
1 cup Bulgur	2 cups	20 minutes	2½ cups
1 cup Millet	3 cups	45 minutes	3½ cups
1 cup Rolled Oats	1½ cups	15 minutes	2½ cups
1 cup Whole Wheat	2 cups	1 hour	2½ cups

Helpful Hints for Cooking Grains

- ½ teaspoon Blackstrap molasses (helps increase mineral content)
- Use a variety of sweeteners (don't use the same ones every time)
- Other ingredients to add to grains:
- Flaxseed — adds fiber and nutty flavor
- Coconut — rich in calcium
- Vanilla — adds flavor and aids in digestion
- Dried fruit — natural sweetener

For faster grain preparation, try the thermos method:

1 wide mouth quart thermos	Sweetener
1 cup grain	2 cups boiling water

Before bed, combine in thermos. Leave about 1-inch space between the water and the top of the thermos since grains will expand. Serve in the morning.

Breakfast Recipes

(protein powder can be added to any of these drinks for extra nutrition!)

BANANA PINEAPPLE SMOOTHIE

2 sliced bananas	1 teaspoon vanilla
1 cup fresh cut pineapple	½ cup water
1 cup coconut pineapple juice	crushed ice

Peel bananas and freeze. Combine all ingredients in a blender except bananas. Mix well. Add bananas gradually until shake thickens. Add additional bananas to create a thicker consistency. Serve with half pineapple wedge and straw. **Serves 2**.

STRAWBANANA FROSTIE

1 cup frozen strawberries	½ cup water
2 frozen bananas	½ teaspoon cinnamon
1 cup unprocessed apple juice	

Combine sliced bananas and strawberries in bowl. Top with shredded coconut. **Serves 4**.

SPRING FRUIT BOWL

4 sliced bananas   ¼ cup shredded coconut
2 cups fresh strawberries, sliced

Combine sliced bananas and strawberries in bowl. Top with shredded coconut.
Serves 4.

SUMMER FRUIT BOWL

4 cups watermelon, cubed   2 cups honeydew melon balls
  and seeds removed   2 cups cantaloupe balls

Combine all three melons together and top with shredded coconut.
Serves 4.

FALL FRUIT BOWL

2 apples, cored and cubed   3 tablespoon fresh lemon juice
2 pears, cored and cubed   2 peaches, sliced

Combine fruit and add lemon juice. Mix so juice coasts all fruit. **Serves
4 to 6**.

WINTER FRUIT BOWL

2 pink grapefruit   1 cup pineapple, chopped
6 large oranges   ¼ cup coconut

Peel fruit and cut into bite-size pieces. Mix well and top with coconut. **Serves 4**.

BROWN RICE BREAKFAST PUDDING

2 cups milk

4 yard eggs, beaten

½ cup fructose

3 cups cooked brown rice

½ teaspoon blackstrap molasses

2 teaspoons vanilla

2 teaspoons cinnamon

Preheat oven to 350°. In blender mix together ½ cup cooked rice until it becomes creamy. [a7] Mix together all liquid ingredients including eggs and creamy rice mixture. Stir in cinnamon. Add rice. Pour into buttered baking dish. Bake 1 hour. Tastes great hot or cold.

HOT NUTTY QUINOA

1 cup quinoa*

2 cups water

2 tablespoons maple syrup

¼ cup unsweetened coconut

1 teaspoon cinnamon

½ cup finely chopped almonds

Rinse quinoa thoroughly. Bring water to a boil. Stir in quinoa. Reduce heat to low and add remaining ingredients. Simmer on low for 15 minutes. **Serves 2 to 3**.

*Quinoa is a "super grain" found in whole food markets.

MILLET CEREAL

3 cups water

1 cup millet

½ teaspoon blackstrap molasses

2 tablespoons maple syrup

1 apple, finely chopped

1 teaspoon corn oil

2 teaspoons vanilla

1 teaspoon cinnamon

Bring water to a boil. Add millet and reduce heat. Add remaining ingredients and simmer for 40 minutes. **Serves 2 to 4.**

BANANA FRENCH TOAST

1 cup low fat milk

4 eggs

1 teaspoon cinnamon

½ teaspoon vanilla

1 ripe banana, thinly sliced

8 slices whole wheat bread

Combine eggs, milk, cinnamon and vanilla. Add bananas. Dip each slice of bread in egg mixture. Bake in oiled skillet or on hot griddle until both sides are golden brown. Serve with maple syrup. **Serves 4**.

SWISS OMELET

2 tablespoons olive oil

½ cup minced onion

6 eggs

¼ cup milk

Dash of salt

½ cup green pepper, finely chopped

½ cup grated swiss cheese

Beat together eggs, milk, and salt. Pour into oiled skillet and cook on medium heat until omelet sets. Lift up edges. Add vegetables to center and sprinkle with cheese. Fold omelet. Remove from heat. **Serves 2 to 4**.

BLUEBERRY BUCKWHEAT PANCAKES

1½ cups buckwheat flour

¼ cup pastry flour or
    whole wheat flour

½ teaspoon baking powder

¾ teaspoon baking soda

1 teaspoon cinnamon

2 tablespoons melted butter

2 eggs, separated

2 teaspoons vanilla

1½ cups buttermilk

½ cup fresh or frozen blueberries

In large bowl, combine first 5 ingredients. Mix well. In small stainless bowl beat egg whites until they peak. In separate bowl lightly beat egg yolks. Add buttermilk, vanilla, oil, and beaten egg white. Mix with flour mixture. Fold in blueberries. Bake on griddle, browning both sides. **Serves 6**.

BLUEBERRY SYRUP

2 cups unsweetened frozen blueberries   ½ cup maple syrup
1 cup blueberry preserves

Place partially thawed blueberries in blender until mashed. Pour blueberries in saucepan with preserves and syrup; cook over low heat. Serve hot over pancakes.

FAMILY GRANOLA

½ cup water   1 cup sunflower seeds
½ cup sorghum   1½ cups unsweetened coconut
½ cup maple syrup   1 cup chopped pecans
¼ cup corn oil   1 cup chopped walnuts
2 teaspoons vanilla   1 teaspoon cinnamon
6 cups rolled oats   Dried fruit (optional)

Combine all dry ingredients in large bowl and mix well. Mix all liquid ingredients well and add to dry ingredients until coated. Spread on large roasting pan. Bake at 325° for 20 to 30 minutes [a8] stirring every 10 to 15 minutes for even browning. Store in refrigerator in airtight containers. Serve as a cereal or snack. **Serves 8**.

THREE SEED GRANOLA

(high in Omega 3 fatty acids)

½ cup sunflower seeds   ½ cup flax seeds
½ cup unhulled sesame seeds   ¼ cup maple syrup

In mini grinder (or coffee grinder) grind each half cup of seeds. Mix together in a small bowl. Heat syrup to help it mix easier. Add syrup to seeds. Stir until seeds are completely coated. **Serves 2**.

MINI BRAN MUFFINS

1 cup boiling water

2 cups wheat bran

2½ cups whole wheat flour

1½ teaspoons baking soda

1 tablespoon cinnamon

½ cup butter

½ cup fructose

2 eggs, beaten

1 cup buttermilk

½ teaspoon vanilla

1 cup chopped pecans

Add boiling water to bran; mix well and set aside. In large bowl mix together eggs, oil, buttermilk, and vanilla. In smaller bowl mix together flour, soda, cinnamon, and fructose. Stir in bran with liquid ingredients. Stir in flour mixture and mix well. Spoon batter into mini cupcake tins. (I prefer to use individual cupcake liners.) Bake at 350° for 15 to 20 minutes. This bran muffin batter can be stored in refrigerator for several days. Bake as needed. This is a great recipe for company. **Yields 48 muffins**.

BREAKFAST GRAIN MUFFINS

¾ cup skim milk

3 tablespoons melted butter

1¾ cups rolled oats

½ cup whole wheat flour

1 tablespoon cinnamon

¼ cup sorghum

½ cup fructose

1 egg beaten

1 teaspoon vanilla

2 teaspoons baking powder

½ cup chopped dates

½ cup chopped pecans

Sift flour and mix with rolled oats and fructose. Stir in baking powder, nuts, dates and cinnamon. Mix together milk, butter, and vanilla. Add flour mixture. Fill muffin tins ⅔ full and bake in hot oven at 400° for 20 minutes. **Serves 12**.

HAWAIIAN CREAM OF WHEAT

1 cup bulgar wheat

2 cups water

¼ cup milk

2 tablespoons fructose

¼ teaspoon blackstrap molasses

¼ cup dried pineapple, chopped

¼ cup unsweetened coconut

½ tablespoon cinnamon

1 teaspoon vanilla

Bring water to boil. Add ingredients one at a time, adding bulgur last. Cover and simmer for 20 minutes. Serve immediately. **Serves 4**.

BROCCOLI QUICHE

8 eggs

2 cups white cheddar cheese, grated

½ teaspoon nutmeg

½ teaspoon sea salt

Mix together all ingredients.

Stir in:

1 package frozen spinach,
thawed and drained (optional)

1 package frozen broccoli, thawed

1 large onion, chopped

Pour quiche into pie crust and bake at 350° for 30 to 40 minutes or when inserted knife comes out clean.

QUICK PIE CRUST

1 package of Arrowhead all purpose Mix

BAKED OATMEAL

⅓ cup butter
1 large egg, beaten
1½ teaspoons baking powder
¾ cup milk

¼ cup fructose
1½ cups rolled oats
¼ teaspoon salt

Preheat oven to 350°. Beat butter, fructose, and eggs together. Add remaining ingredients. Pour into greased 9-by-5-inch pan. Bake at 350° for 45 minutes.

HOT APPLES AND OATS

3 cups water
2 cups unprocessed rolled oats
½ cup fresh or dried apples, chopped

⅛ teaspoon blackstrap molasses
2 tablespoon fructose
½ tablespoon cinnamon

Bring water to a boil. Add all ingredients, adding oats last. Cover and simmer for 5 minutes. Remove from heat and let stand for 5 minutes. **Serves 6**.

BLUEBERRY MUFFINS

2 yard eggs
1 cup whole wheat flour
2 cups whole wheat pastry flour
¼ cup maple syrup
¼ cup fructose
1½ cups buttermilk

¼ cup raw butter
1 teaspoon baking soda
½ teaspoon baking powder
1 teaspoon vanilla
1 teaspoon cinnamon
1 cup fresh blueberries

In blender combine butter and sweeteners. Add eggs, buttermilk, and vanilla. In large bowl mix together flours, baking soda, baking powder, and cinnamon. Stir in blender mixture. Mix well. Stir in blueberries. Bake at 350° in greased and floured muffin tins for 30 minutes.

NOTES

Valuable Vegetables

Main Dishes
Side Dishes

3

Valuable Vegetables

Too many of us think of vegetables as a side show. Not so! They are at the center-stage of our nutritional health. Vegetables are delicious, interesting, and perfectly able to carry the nightly dinner show all by themselves if called up to do so. We've given vegetables second billing for far too long.

I guarantee that if your personal attitude reflects the respect that these nutritional marvels deserve, your family's attitudes will follow.

Be creative, inventive, and even artistic in the way you think about, select, prepare, and present valuable vegetables. Don't be afraid to try new varieties. Most people eat the same ten to twelve kinds of vegetables day after day and year after year. It's no wonder they get bored with them. The Lord has given us over 150 plus different vegetables to choose. Nothing is more interesting, colorful, delicious, and delightful than a well prepared vegetable dish!

During World War II, families were encouraged to supplement their food supply by growing vegetables in "Victory Gardens" in their backyards. Families patriotically supported the war effort and, as a side benefit, enjoyed very nourishing, healthy meals. Since then, the average American family has lost its love for vegetables and, unfortunately, has suffered the loss of a measure of good health.

[a12] What we are served at fast foods restaurants has had a tremendous impact on our eating habits in the last twenty to thirty years. Very few people still grow their own vegetables, while others simply neglect to include them in their daily diets.

Vegetables give our bodies a variety of vitamins, minerals, and proteins from which to build healthy cells and supply energy. All vegetables are quickly and easily digested, which makes them low-stress foods, meaning the body does not have to work hard to digest them. My family agrees that we feel better when we eat more vegetables throughout the week. Plan to enjoy a variety of vegetables every day.

Purchasing Vegetables

I often wonder if some grocers cringe when they see us coming. We are the discriminating vegetable buyers who carefully inspect each item. We squeeze squash, peek into the folded husks of the ears of corn, turn up the hidden sides of peppers, and have been caught making faces before returning an unripe tomato to its peers. If you are not a vegetable squeezer, I encourage you to join the fun!

Fresh is best when it comes to purchasing vegetables. However, fresh isn't always possible or the most cost effective approach. The following are some practical guidelines for purchasing vegetables.

Why Organic?

Organic fruits and vegetables are grown without insecticides, pesticides, weed killers, and other toxic chemicals. I have grown increasingly adamant about the need to eat organically grown foods. I do realize the cost is a deciding factor for most shoppers — it used to be my first priority, too. But as I have learned more about the chemicals and additives in our food over the years, I have become more committed to "creative spending" for the sake of my family's good health.

Have you ever tallied up the amount of money you spend on junk food in a week? With a little creativity you can begin buying organic foods, purchase less junk food, and still save money! Why not try it? This cookbook is filled with healthy, nutritious recipes to satisfy your family's snacking requests.

More and more consumers are going organic and production is on the increase. Modern farmers are resisting these destructive, unhealthy planting methods and are insisting on keeping their soil alive and productive. In addition, the demand is rising for foods grown without toxic chemicals. If you are going to start buying organic fruits and vegetables, start replacing the items that usually have the highest amounts of pesticide residues: apples, strawberries, broccoli, peaches, grapes, pears, spinach.

For your family's sake, find places in your food budget where you can cut costs and use the savings toward organically grown food whenever possible.

Fresh

- Always try to buy vegetables that are in season.
- Fresh vegetables should be purchased at a farmer's market, private stand, or co-op whenever possible.

- Always wash vegetables with a biodegradable cleanser. This will strip off water-repellent chemicals and wax. When washed properly, in most cases, the skin and peeling can be consumed.
- When you have a choice, buy organic. Organic vegetables are usually larger in size, fresher, and more flavorful. Most importantly, they are supposed to be free of harmful chemicals.

Frozen

Vitamins are lost in the freezing of vegetables but the minerals are still available. Home-grown frozen vegetables are much better than those purchased in grocery stores. If you do buy frozen vegetables from your grocer, look for the brands with nothing added.

Canned

Try to use non-organic commercially canned vegetables as little as possible. Almost all canned vegetables have too much salt and sugar added. In addition, the canning process tends to rob vegetables of much of their nutritional value, I try to buy organic varieties in coated (non-aluminum) cans.

Buying Guide — Fresh Vegetables And Fruits

Experience is the best teacher in choosing quality, but here are a few pointers that may help you select the best fruits and vegetables.

Asparagus — The stalks should be tender and firm, and the tips should be close and compact. Choose the stalks with very little white — they are the most tender. Eat asparagus right away because it tends to toughen quickly.

Beans, Snap Beans — Choose beans with small seeds inside the pods. Avoid beans with dry-looking pods.

Berries — Select plump, solid berries with good color. Avoid stained containers, which indicate wet or leaky berries. Berries such as blackberries and raspberries with clinging caps may be under ripe. Strawberries without caps may be too ripe.

Broccoli, Brussels Sprouts and Cauliflower — Flower cluster on broccoli and cauliflower should be tight and close together. Brussels sprouts should be firm and compact. Smudgy, dirty spots may indicate that insects are hiding inside.

Cabbage and Head lettuce — Hold the heads in your hand and feel them for weight. Choose heads that feel heavy for size. Avoid cabbage with worm holes, and lettuce with any discoloration or soft rot.

Cucumbers — Choose long, slender cucumbers for best quality. Fresh cukes can be dark or medium green, but yellowed ones are undesirable.

Melons — Thick close netting on cantaloupe rind indicates the best quality. A cantaloupe is ripe when the stem scar is smooth and the space between the netting is yellow or yellow-green. They taste best when they are fully ripe with a fruity odor. Honeydews are ripe when the rind has a creamy to yellowish color and a velvety texture. Immature honeydews are whitish-green. Ripe watermelons have some yellow color on one side. But if they are white or pale green on one side, they are not ripe.

Orange, Grapefruit, and Lemons — Pick up the citrus fruit and feel it for weight. Choose fruit that is heavy for its size. Smoother, thicker skins usually indicate more juice. Most skin markings do not indicate the fruits quality. Oranges with a slight greenish tinge may be just as ripe as fully colored ones. Light or greenish-yellow lemons are more tart than deep yellow ones. Avoid citrus fruits showing withered, sunken, or soft areas.

Peas and Lima Beans — Select pods that are well-fitted but not bulging. Avoid dried, spotted, yellowed, or flabby pods.

Root Vegetables — Pick them up and squeeze them. Root vegetables should be smooth and firm. Very large carrots may have woody cores, oversized radishes may be pithy and oversized turnips, beets and parsnips may be woody. Fresh carrot tops usually indicate fresh carrots, but the condition of leaves on most other root vegetables does not indicate degree of freshness.

Sweet Potatoes — Puerto Rico and Nancy Hall varieties with bronze to rosy skins are soft and sweet when cooked. Yellow to light brown Jersey types are firmer and less moist.

Vegetables — Think Creatively!

Vegetable lovers must develop a creative sense of discovery. It is important to have as much variety in your family's diet as possible. Which vegetables do you eat on a regular basis? Which ones have you tried only once or twice? Note all the vegetables you have never tried. Why not? Can you think of some creative ways to discover these valuable vegetables?

Green Leafy:

Beet greens	Leaf lettuce
Brussels Sprouts	Mustard greens
Cabbage	Romaine lettuce
Collards	Spinach
Kale	Turnip greens
Dandelion greens	

Manganese:

Avocado	Okra
Corn	Peppers
Cucumber	Squash
Eggplant	Tomatoes

Root:

Beets	Rutabaga
Carrots	Sweet Potatoes
Horseradish	Turnips
Jerusalem Artichokes	White potatoes
Parsnips	Yams
Radishes	

Yellow:

Acorn squash	Hubbard squash
Butternut squash	Rutabaga
Buttercup squash	Spaghetti Squash
Carrots	Summer squash
Corn	Sweet potatoes

Miscellaneous:

Artichoke	Mushrooms
Asparagus	Rhubarb
Cauliflower	Sauerkraut
Celery	Water Chestnuts
Hominy	Zucchini
Kohlrabi	

Preparing Vegetables

Vegetables only become boring when chefs get bored with them. Preparation makes all the difference in the world! You may dislike a certain vegetable, but discover, if prepared differently, it tastes absolutely delightful. Be creative!

The recipes in this chapter include certain vegetables that have been prepared in different ways. I know you'll enjoy finding special favorites that appeal to the individual tastes of your family members. Below are the basic vegetable preparation methods. Try them all, and discover which ones your family enjoys best.

Raw Vegetables

Raw vegetables can help to rapidly detoxify the body. Because of their high fiber content, they can keep the intestinal tract swept clean and are sometimes called "intestinal brooms." If your digestive system is in good working condition, raw vegetables are great for you.

Juicing Vegetables

Drinking fresh vegetable juice is the best way to receive important needed enzymes, vitamins, and minerals. Juices are easily digested and add variety to your diet. What vegetables should you juice? Start with these terrific ones: carrots, cabbage, celery, and parsley.

Carrots are very high in beta carotene, which is a natural source of vitamin A. Juices benefit us most when we drink them daily. Keep them sealed tightly in the refrigerator because they can lose their nutritional value when exposed to air. Be creative and mix several juices together for variety. (See appendix for juicer information.)

Steaming Vegetables

Steaming is another way to prepare vegetables. Foldable stainless steel steamers can be purchased at your local grocery store.

Directions for steaming: Place ½ to 1 inch of water in pot. Place vegetables in steamer. Bring water to a boil, cover, and reduce heat. Steam until tender (not mushy).

Summering Vegetables

It is best to start with very little water when cooking vegetables, and add more water later if needed.

Stir-Fry Vegetables

Stir-frying is my favorite way of preparing vegetables. You don't need to purchase a wok in order to stir-fry vegetables. I do all my stir-frying in a cast iron skillet, but you may find it fun to buy an inexpensive one. If you do use a wok, the best type is stainless steel.

Advantages of stir-frying:

- It's the best way to prepare a balanced vegetable dish.

- Vegetables retain most of their crispness and are never overcooked.

Vegetables best used in stir-fry:

Onions*	Cabbage
Green peppers	Yellow squash
Celery	Broccoli
Carrots	Zucchini
Pea Pods	Bean sprouts

Extra ingredients for stir-fry:

Sliced water chestnuts	Cashews
Almonds	Chicken breast strips
Sliced bamboo shoots	

* Onions should be cooked first, then set aside. Add at the end when all other vegetables are stir-fried.

Baking Vegetables

Vegetables are often baked in the form of a casserole, except for certain types of squash and sweet potatoes. When baking squash or pumpkins, save the seeds. The seeds make an excellent snack. Just wash them, baste them with a little butter, and bake them on a cookie sheet.

A Whole Lotta Shakin Goin On

Most Americans have a "salt tooth". I certainly did. The best way to get away from the salt shaker is to cut back gradually, giving your taste buds an opportunity to change.

It takes twenty-eight days to break a habit. If you can avoid salt for twenty-eight days, you will be amazed at how much you will enjoy the natural flavor of your food. (Celery tends to have more natural salt than other vegetables.)

The Story Of A Canned Pea

In Dr. Ruben's book, "Everything You Wanted to Know About Food," I enjoyed his story of The Canned Pea and I wanted to share it with you.

The "life of a pea" was studied from the farmer's field to the American dinner table. After the pea arrives at the factory:

- Thirty percent of the nutrients are lost during the cooking and canning process.

- Twenty-five percent of the nutrients are lost in the sterilization process.

- Twenty-seven percent of the nutrients float away in discarded fluids.

- Twelve percent of the nutrients are lost while cooking the peas at home.

What you end up with is a "little round, green disaster" that has lost 94 percent of its nutrients.

BROCCOLI SALAD

1 bunch broccoli, thoroughly washed	½ cup purple onion, chopped
1 cup celery, chopped	½ honey roasted peanuts
¾ cup mayonnaise	⅛ cup fructose
1 tablespoon vinegar	⅛ cup "Bake-ums"
	(soy bacon replacement)

Mix all ingredients, except Bake-ums, and chill in refrigerator several hours. Toss in Bake-ums just before serving.

QUICK CREAMED SPINACH

2 packages frozen spinach, thawed   4 tablespoons low fat cottage cheese
½ teaspoons salt   ½ cup grated cheese

Drain spinach. In blender combine spinach and cottage cheese. Blend well. Pour into large saucepan and add salt and cheese. Stir until cheese has melted. **Serves 4.**

EGGPLANT PARMESAN

2 eggplant, peeled and cut   1 (32 oz.) jar of meatless
   into ½ inch slices   natural spaghetti sauce
3 eggs   ½ teaspoon basil
1 cup whole wheat flour   1 teaspoon garlic powder
1 cup cornmeal   Olive oil
½ teaspoons sea salt (optional)   1 large onion, chopped
1 green pepper, chopped   1 tablespoon tamari sauce
2 tomatoes, chopped   1 cup grated cheese

Combine flour, meal, and salt in a small bowl. Mix eggs in another small bowl. Dip each piece of eggplant in egg, then coat with flour mixture. Place in small amount of oil in skillet. Brown on both sides. Place on paper towel. When finished frying eggplant, sauté onions and pepper in skillet. Add remaining ingredients. Simmer for 10 minutes. Place eggplant in large baking dish. Pour mixture in skillet on top of eggplant and top with grated cheese. Bake at 350° for 30 minutes. **Serves 6**.

VEGGIE TACOS

1 cup soy burger	1 stalk celery, chopped
1 cup water	1 can natural jalapeno bean dip
1 large onion, chopped	2 cups prepared refried beans
1 medium green pepper, chopped	

Saute onion in oil in large skillet. Add green pepper and celery. Cook on medium heat until tender. Add water to soy burger. When water is absorbed, add to vegetables. Add refried beans and jalapeno bean dip. Mix well and cook on low heat for 15 minutes.

8 to 10 whole wheat flour tortillas	1 head leaf lettuce
(or corn taco shells)	1 small onion
1 tomato, chopped	½ cup grated cheddar cheese

Mix together tomato, lettuce, and onion in salad bowl. Heat shells. Spoon bean mixture into shells. Top with lettuce, tomato, and cheese. **Serves 6 to 8**.

SOY MEATBALLS
AND ZUCCHINI ESPANOL

½ cup water	3 cups hot cooked brown rice
1¼ cups soy burger	½ teaspoon garlic powder
1½ cups soft whole wheat	1 tablespoon tamari sauce
bread crumbs	1 tablespoon fresh parsley, chopped
½ onion, finely chopped	1½ cups picante sauce
½ teaspoon worcestershire sauce	1 cup chopped tomato
4 tablespoons whole wheat flour	2½ cups zucchini, thinly sliced

In large mixing bowl combine soy burger and water. Mix well, then add bread crumbs, onion, Worcestershire sauce, flour, garlic, tamari sauce, and parsley. Mix well and form into 16 to 18 (1 inch) meatballs. Place in shallow baking dish. Bake at 375° for 20 minutes. Mix together picante sauce, chopped tomato, and zucchini. Pour over meatballs. Bake 10 minutes and serve over bed of rice. **Serves 6**.

ASPARAGUS WITH BLEU CHEESE

Wash 1 pound fresh asparagus and chop about 1¼ inches off stem bottoms. Cover and place whole asparagus in small amount of water. Bring water to a boil. Reduce heat and simmer for 15 minutes or until tender.

2 tablespoons butter	⅛ teaspoon cayenne pepper
1 tablespoon whole wheat flour	1 cup nonfat milk
½ teaspoon arrowroot	½ cup crumbled bleu cheese

Melt butter. Mix together arrowroot and flour; slowly add to cold milk. Stir in with melted butter. Bring to a simmer and gradually add Bleu cheese. Stir over low heat until thickened. Serve over asparagus. **Serves 4**.

GLAZED CARROTS

8 medium carrots	1 tablespoon fructose
¾ cup water	3 tablespoon fresh orange juice

Simmer carrots in water until almost tender. Remove carrots; add juice and sorghum to carrot water. Bring to a boil and boil for 3 minutes. Add carrots and simmer for 5 minutes. **Serves 6**.

VANILLA AND SPICE CARROTS

3 carrots (medium) sliced	2 tablespoons water
1 tablespoon raw butter	1½ teaspoons vanilla
1 tablespoon sorghum	1½ teaspoons cinnamon

Saute carrots in butter for 2 minutes. Mix together remaining ingredients and pour over carrots. Stir and simmer on low heat for 5 to 10 minutes, until carrots are slightly tender. **Serves 4**.

CREAMED CARROTS

3 tablespoons butter

2 cups thinly sliced carrots

¼ cup cold water

2 tablespoons whole wheat flour

½ teaspoon arrowroot

1 tablespoon tamari sauce

1 teaspoon garlic powder

Saute carrots in corn oil in skillet for 5 minutes. Cover and cook on warm for several minutes more. Mix flour and arrowroot with cold water until smooth. Add garlic and tamari sauce to water. Pour over carrots; stir and mix well. Cook on low for 2 minutes. **Serves 4**.

STUFFED GREEN PEPPERS

1 pound ground beef

6 green bell peppers

1 cup natural picante sauce

½ teaspoon basil

1 medium onion, chopped

1 cup cooked brown rice

1 cup cooked corn

2 tablespoons fresh parsley, chopped

½ cup shredded cheddar cheese

Clean peppers, cut off tops, and remove seeds. Simmer in water for 15 minutes, making sure not to over cook. In large skillet, sauté onion and brown beef. Drain any grease. Add remaining ingredients. Stuff peppers and top with cheese. Bake at 350° for 25 minutes.

CARROT MILLET BURGERS

3 tablespoons corn oil

3 cups cooked millet

1 small onion, finely chopped

½ cup grated carrots

½ cup whole wheat flour

1 tablespoon tamari sauce

⅛ teaspoon worcestershire sauce

1 teaspoon garlic powder

1 teaspoon fresh parsley, chopped

1 teaspoon basil

Coat skillet with oil. Mix all ingredients together. Make into patties. Cook on medium heat, browning both sides. Top with mushroom gravy. **Serves 6**.

SUPER VEGGIE SUPPER

2 tablespoons olive oil

1 clove garlic, minced

½ teaspoon dried oregano

1 tablespoon Tamari sauce

1 small onion, chopped

1 medium green pepper, chopped

1½ cups zucchini, sliced

⅛ teaspoon cayenne pepper

2 cups chopped tomatoes

2 cups kidney beans, cooked

2½ cups grated cheddar cheese

2½ cups cooked brown rice

In large skillet, sauté onion and garlic in oil. Add green pepper, zucchini, oregano, and cayenne pepper. Cook until vegetables are tender, about 5 minutes. Add tamari sauce, tomatoes, and beans. Cover and cook on low for 3 to 5 minutes. Serve vegetables over brown rice and top with cheese. **Serves 4**.

SWISS VEGETABLES

1 head cauliflower

2 cups broccoli florets

2 medium carrots, sliced

1 package natural dry mushroom soup mix

⅓ cup plain raw yogurt

1 cup grated Swiss cheese

¾ cup water

Mix dry soup with water. Add this to yogurt and ½ cup of cheese. Steam vegetables and mix in with soup mixture. Pour in casserole dish. Cover and bake for 30 minutes. Top with remaining cheese and bake, uncovered, 5 more minutes. **Serves 6**.

MUSTARD GREENS AND GARLIC

2 pounds mustard greens

½ cup water

2 tablespoons olive oil with garlic

1 teaspoon tamari sauce

Cut leaves from stems of mustard greens. Wash leaves and chop into bite-size pieces. Put oil in 4½ quart pot. Add mustard greens and mix well to coat leaves with oil. Cook on low heat for 10 minutes in oil. Gradually add water. Cover and simmer for 15 to 20 minutes, until leaves are a dark green. Drain and serve as a side dish. **Serves 4 to 6**.

COOKED KALE

2 heads kale (purple or green)
2 tablespoons olive oil with garlic

1 small onion, chopped
1 teaspoon tamari sauce

Prepare kale the same way as the mustard greens (see preceding), but add onions at the same time the oil is added. Simmer only for 10 minutes. **Serves 4**.

COLLARD GREENS

1 pound collard greens
½ cup water

1 tablespoon olive oil with garlic
1 teaspoon tamari sauce

Prepare collard greens the same way the mustard greens are prepared (see preceding). **Serves 4**.

GLAZED BEETS

2½ cups fresh beets, sliced
2 tablespoons butter

¼ cup unsweetened apricot preserves

Wash, peel, and slice beets. Cover and cook in small amount of water for 20 minutes; drain. In skillet, melt butter and stir in preserves. Add beets. Stir and cook on low for 2 minutes. **Serves 4**.

BROCCOLI SIDE DISH

2 heads broccoli
2 tablespoons butter
2 tablespoons fresh lemon juice

½ teaspoon garlic powder
¼ teaspoon basil

Cut large stems off of broccoli. Wash, then steam broccoli for about 15 minutes. Simmer remaining ingredients. Drain broccoli and pour lemon mixture over broccoli. **Serves 6**.

BRUSSELS SPROUTS WITH ALMONDS

1 pound brussels sprouts
1 cup chopped almonds
3 tablespoons butter

Juice of 2 lemons
Walnuts or pecans (also work well)

Wash Brussels sprouts. Cut off bottoms and cut an "x" in the bottom of each one. Simmer Brussels sprouts until tender. Brown almonds in butter, then add lemon juice. Drain sprouts and top with nuts. Serve immediately. **Serves 6**.

PEA PODS IN GRAVY

3 cups fresh pea pods
¼ cup slivered almonds
¼ cup fresh mushrooms, sliced
2 tablespoons butter

⅓ cup water
2 tablespoons tamari sauce
1 teaspoon arrowroot

Melt butter in skillet. Add almonds and brown on low heat. Add pea pods and stir-fry for 2 to 3 minutes. Stir in mushrooms. In small bowl, mix together water, tamari sauce, and arrowroot. Stir sauce in gradually with pea pods until thickened. **Serves 4**.

SQUASH AND ONIONS

3 medium yellow squash, thinly sliced
1 medium onion, sliced

1 tablespoon olive oil with garlic
½ teaspoon salt

Saute squash and onion in oil. Add tamari sauce and stir. Stir-fry for 3 to 5 minutes. **Serves 4**.

YELLOW SQUASH CASSEROLE

5 medium summer squash, grated

1 medium carrot, chopped

1 medium green pepper, chopped

2 eggs

1 cup whole wheat bread crumbs

1 cup Swiss cheese, grated

1 teaspoon garlic powder

1 teaspoon coriander

1 tablespoon fresh parsley, chopped

½ teaspoon salt

Mix together all ingredients except ½ cup of grated cheese. Pour in 2 quart casserole dish; top with remaining cheese. Bake at 350° for 30 minutes. **Serves 6**.

ITALIAN ZUCCHINI

1 cup fresh corn, cut

2 tomatoes, chopped

1 medium zucchini, thinly sliced

¼ cup shredded swiss cheese

½ teaspoon Italian seasoning

¼ cup water

Bring to boil water, corn, tomatoes, and seasoning. Reduce heat and cook for 3 minutes. Stir in zucchini and cook for 5 minutes. Top with cheese and serve. **Serves 4**.

SPAGHETTI SQUASH

1 spaghetti sauce (large)

2 tablespoons raw butter

2 tablespoons Parmesan cheese

Squash

Cut off ends of squash and slice in half. Spoon out seeds and carve off outside peeling. Cut into 2 inch pieces. Place in large saucepan and cover with water. Bring to a boil, then simmer for 20 minutes or until squash starts falling apart and looks like spaghetti. Drain well. Stir in butter and top with cheese. This can also be used as a noodles served with spaghetti sauce. **Serves 4**.

BAKED SWEET POTATOES

4 medium sweet potatoes scrubbed   1 tablespoon butter
2 tablespoons fructose   ½ cup water

Slice potatoes into ¼ inch pieces and lay in baking dish. Pour water over potatoes. Melt butter and mix with fructose. Pour over potatoes. Cover and bake at 350° for 1 hour. **Serves 8**.

ALMOND BUTTER AND SWEET POTATOES

4 medium sweet potatoes   1 teaspoon fructose
4 tablespoons almond butter

Cut potatoes in half so you don't have a boat shape. Boil until tender. Mix almond butter and fructose until smooth. A little water may be added if needed to make smoother. Place potato halves in shallow baking dish. Cut a small trench in center of potatoes and spread on almond mixture. Bake for 15 minutes at 325°. **Serves 8**.

MASHED SWEET POTATOES

4 medium sweet potatoes,   ⅛ teaspoon orange peel, grated
   peeled and cubed   2 tablespoons fructose
1 tablespoon butter   ½ teaspoon cinnamon

Boil sweet potatoes with orange peel in water until tender. Drain potatoes. Whip potatoes with electric mixer. Beat in butter and remaining ingredients until creamy. Place in baking dish and top with Meringue (following recipe).

MERINGUE

3 egg whites	½ teaspoon vanilla
3 tablespoons fructose	

In stainless steel bowl mix egg whites and vanilla with electric mixer at high speed. When meringue starts to peak, add fructose slowly. Beat for 3 more minutes, then spread over sweet potatoes. Bake at 325° until meringue starts to lightly brown. **Serves 6**.

STUFFED SWEET POTATOES

6 medium sweet potatoes	1 egg
Butter	¼ cup butter
¼ cup sorghum	¼. teaspoons cinnamon
½ teaspoon allspice	¼ cup pecans, chopped

Wash potatoes and rub with butter. Bake at 375° for 1 hour. Slice off top of each potato and carefully scoop out pulp, leaving an empty shell. Mash pulp and mix in remaining ingredients. Bake at 350° for 10 minutes. **Serves 6**.

SPINACH-ZUCCHINI LASAGNA

3 tablespoons olive oil	2 medium zucchini, thinly sliced
1 clove garlic, minced	1 medium green pepper
1 large onion, chopped	

In skillet, sauté garlic and onion in oil. Add zucchini and green pepper. Cook on low heat until tender. Add mushrooms. Set aside.

1 (32 oz.) jar natural spaghetti sauce	1 (16 oz.) container low-fat
2 eggs, slightly beaten	cottage cheese

Stir spaghetti sauce in with vegetables. Simmer for 5 minutes. In bowl, mix together eggs and cottage cheese. Set aside.

4 cups fresh spinach	1 cup Mozzarella cheese, grated
1 (8 oz.) box artichoke lasagna noodles	

Cook noodles following package directions. Wash spinach and remove stems. Oil bottom of 13-by-9 inch baking dish. Start layering lasagna with a little sauce on bottom, then noodles, then cottage cheese, then spinach, then vegetables with sauce, then cheese. Repeat layers in same order. Top with remaining cheese. Back at 350° for 45 minutes. **Serves 4 to 6**.

LASAGNA ROLL-UPS

3 tablespoons olive oil with garlic	¾ cups water
1 large onion, chopped	2 eggs
1 medium red bell pepper chopped	2 (15 oz.) containers ricotta cheese
1 medium green bell pepper, chopped	1 cup natural bottled spaghetti
1 pound ground beef	2 teaspoons garlic powder
2 boxes artichoke lasagna noodles	1½ packages frozen spinach

In large skillet sauté onion and oil. Add beef. When beef is browned, drain fat and add peppers. Simmer until peppers are slightly cooked. In large bowl mix eggs and ricotta cheese. Stir in spinach. Place cooked noodles flat in a greased 9-by-14-inch baking dish. Spoon cheese mixture on individual noodles, then roll noodles. If noodle will not stay rolled, insert toothpick. Continue same procedure with each noodle until there are three rows of lasagna noodles (6 to 7 rolls in each row). Pour spaghetti sauce over each row and top with Mozzarella cheese. Bake at 350° for 30 minutes. **Serves 6 to 8**.

STUFFED SPINACH SHELLS

1 box jumbo pasta shells	1 cup Mozzarella cheese, grated
2 boxes chopped spinach	2 tablespoons minced garlic
1 large onion, finely chopped	½ teaspoon salt
1 (12 oz.) container cottage cheese	1½ cups pasta sauce
1 (15 oz.) container Ricotta cheese	1 cup grated Parmesan cheese

Cook shells following directions on box. In large bowl combine remaining ingredients except Parmesan cheese and pasta sauce. Mix well. Stuff each cooked shell with about 2 heaping tablespoons of cheese mixture. Oil large casserole dish. Place each stuffed shell open side down. Spread pasta sauce evenly over top of shells. Sprinkle Parmesan cheese over sauce. Bake at 350°, uncovered, for 30 minutes or until cheese has completely melted and sides start to bubble.

VEGGIE STIR FRY

4 tablespoons olive oil	1 can water chestnuts, sliced
1 medium onion, chopped	and drained
1 clove garlic, minced	½ cup water
1 medium bell pepper, cut in strips	1 tablespoon arrowroot or
2 stalks celery, cut in strips	3 tablespoons tamari sauce
2 cups pea pods	1 medium carrot, sliced

Saute onion and garlic in oil and set aside. Add carrot and celery; stir for 1 minute on medium heat. Add bell pepper and stir for 1 minute. Add pea pods, water chestnuts, and onion. Mix arrowroot in water until smooth, then add tamari sauce. Pour over veggies and stir for 2 to 3 minutes. Serve over brown rice. **Serves 4**.

RAMEN STIR FRY

Ramen (quick cooking Japanese pasta noodles):

2 packages (2.8 oz.) Ramen noodles	1 medium onion, finely chopped
1 tablespoon olive oil	2 tablespoons tamari sauce

Cook Ramen in boiling water and rinse with cold water; set aside. Saute onion in olive oil.

2 medium grated carrots	1 medium tomato, finely chopped
1½ cups broccoli, finely chopped	

Add remaining vegetables to onion and cook 5 minutes. Add noodles to vegetables. Mix well. Add tamari sauce and cook for 3 more minutes. Serve immediately. **Serves 4**.

VALERIE'S CORN CASSEROLE

1 tablespoon oil	1 teaspoons chili powder
1 large onion, chopped	1 tablespoon whole wheat flour
¼ cup bell pepper, chopped	3 cups milk
1 cup cut corn	1 cup yellow grits
1 cup cooked pinto beans	1 cup white Cheddar cheese
½ teaspoons cumin	⅛ teaspoon sea salt (optional)

Saute onion and next 5 ingredients in oil. Melt butter in medium size saucepan. Stir in flour; add milk, then grits. Stir on medium to low heat until thick. Stir in sautéed vegetables, cheese, and salt. Bake in casserole dish at 350° for 30 to 40 minutes.

Spice It Up!

You'll find that you can travel from France to Germany to Italy and China with a creative sprinkle of spices, herbs, and seasonings. Listed are popular flavorings for vegetables.

Garlic	Parsley
Onions	Basil
Garlic Powder	Nutmeg
Tamari sauce	Curry
Dill	Sage
Oregano	Dried mustard

MY OWN SPECIAL VEGGIE SEASONING

Try using this to season your vegetables when cooking (this is a good replacement for the flavor that bacon give vegetables.)

1 medium onion	1 cup water
2 stalks celery	

Puree in blender and add water. Plan ahead . . . triple the above recipe. Pour in plastic ice trays and store in the freezer until needed.

GARLIC SEASONING

3 cloves garlic, minced	1 large bottle olive oil

Place minced garlic in bottle of olive oil. The longer you leave the garlic in the oil to marinate, the stronger the flavor will become.

Herb Guide

Basil

FOUND IN: India, Western Europe, United States

IT IS: member of mint family with leaves 1½ inches long; has mild aromatic odor; warm, sweet flavor with slight licorice taste

TASTES GOOD WITH: tomatoes, peas, squash, lamb, fish, eggs, tossed salad, cheese, duck, potatoes

AVAILABLE: whole, ground

Bay Leaf

FOUND IN: Turkey, Yugoslavia, Portugal, Greece

IT IS: green, aromatic leaf of laurel tree, has pungent flavor

TASTES GOOD WITH: vegetables and fish soups, tomato sauces and juice, poached fish, meat stews

AVAILABLE: as whole leaf

Chervil

FOUND IN: France, United States

TASTES GOOD WITH: poultry stuffing, veal and lamb roasts, potatoes, cauliflower, fish, duck

AVAILABLE: whole, ground

Marjoram

FOUND IN: France, Germany, Chile

IT IS: member of mint family, with aromatic odor

TASTES GOOD WITH: fish, vegetable soups, eggs, cheese dishes, stews, roast chicken, beef, lamb, stuffings

AVAILABLE: whole, ground

Sage

FOUND IN: Yugoslavia, Italy, Greece, Spain

IT IS: shrub of mint family, with pleasant aromatic odor and warm, slightly bitter taste

TASTES GOOD WITH: stuffings, poultry, and hamburgers

AVAILABLE: as leaf, rubbed, powdered

Fennel

FOUND IN: India, France, Argentina

IT IS: dried fruit of herb in parsley family, consists of tiny yellowish-brown seeds with licorice flavor

IT IS: member of parsley family with feathery leaves, has mild, delicate flavor

TASTES GOOD WITH: egg and cheese dishes, chicken, peas, spinach, green salads, cream soups

AVAILABLE: whole, ground

Oregano

FOUND IN: Mexico, Italy, Chile, France

IT IS: member of mint family, light-green in color, with strong, aromatic odor and pleasantly bitter taste

TASTES GOOD WITH: tomato sauces, veal dishes, pizza, vegetable and fish salads, chili

AVAILABLE: whole, ground

Mint

FOUND IN: all parts of the world

IT IS: dried leaf of peppermint or spearmint plant, with strong, sweet odor and tangy, cool taste

TASTES GOOD WITH: jellies, fruit juices, candies, frosting, cakes, pies, lamb, ice cream, potatoes, peas, and chocolate desserts

AVAILABLE: whole (dried), flaked, as fresh sprigs

Rosemary

FOUND IN: France, Spain, Portugal

IT IS: leaf of evergreen shrub, with appearance of cured pine needles, aromatic color with slightly pine taste

TASTES GOOD IN: soups, fish dishes, sauces, sweet pickles, bread, and rolls

AVAILABLE: whole, ground

Tarragon

FOUND IN: France, United States

IT IS: leaf and flower-top of plant, has pungent flavor resembling licorice

TASTES GOOD WITH: fish sauces, egg and cheese dishes, green salads, pickles, vinegar, chicken, tomatoes, sauces for meats and vegetables

AVAILABLE: whole, ground

Thyme

FOUND IN: France, Spain

IT IS: member of mint family, with short brown leaves, has warm, aromatic odor, pungent flavor

TASTES GOOD WITH: soups, stuffing, beef, lamb, veal, eggs, cheese, bean and vegetable soups, fish

AVAILABLE: whole, powdered

Parsley

FOUND IN: United States, Europe

IT IS: tiny green leaf growing in clusters on low plant, mild, slightly tangy flavor

TASTES GOOD WITH: meat, vegetables, soups, eggs, cheese

AVAILABLE: whole, ground, as flakes

Savory

> FOUND IN: France, Spain
>
> IT IS: member of mint family and has aromatic odor, pungent flavor
>
> TASTES GOOD WITH: eggs, meat, salads, chicken, soups, stuffing
>
> AVAILABLE: whole, ground

Dill

> FOUND IN: India, United States
>
> IT IS: fruit of parsley family, has aromatic odor with delicate caraway flavor
>
> TASTES GOOD WITH: fish dishes, cream and cottage cheese, potatoes, fish and vegetable salads, pickles, tomatoes
>
> AVAILABLE: whole, ground

Here Are Some More Vegetable Tips!

Increasing Mineral Content: Add ⅛ teaspoon of blackstrap molasses to any cooking water to increase the mineral contents of what you are cooking.

Leftover Vegetables:

- Use in soups
- Add to millet or soy burgers

Soup Starters: Never throw out clean vegetable water after cooking vegetables. The water can be used later for soup starters and chili.

NOTES

Meat, Fish
and Poultry

4

Meat, Fish and Poultry

This is a brief overview of this industry. For more detailed information call our office at 1-800-592-heal and order my husband's best selling, *Maximum Energy* book.

What if you purchased a pork roast at your local grocery store, turned it over, and read:"Warning, the use of this product may be hazardous to your health?" well, someday you may. Pork commonly contains parasites. [professor Hans-heinrich Reckeiveg, M.D. "The Adverse Influence of Pork Consumption on Health,"biological therapy, vol. One, num.Two, 1983.] These meats also digest too quickly for the human metabolism, thereby causing a rapid rise in blood urea. When this occurs, the blood system becomes overloaded, creating excessive stress upon the heart and other organs.

Often, shellfish contain extremely high levels of toxic minerals and parasites, as well, which assault the human immune system. Here in Florida where I live, individuals die on a regular basis from eating these ocean favorites. The Bible considers both pork and shellfish to be"unclean foods". We must remember that shellfish and other types of unclean fish are in the water for a purpose. They are scavenger feeders who eat the debris and eliminated waste of other fish.

God, who created pork and shellfish, warned his people through the Bible about the dangers of these foods. Unclean meats were strictly forbidden in the Old Testament. Here is a list of clean and unclean foods from Leviticus chapter 11.

Red Meat:
> Clean: beef, lamb, mutton, veal
>
> Unclean: pork, dog, cat, horse, mule

Wild Game:
> Clean: buffalo, caribou, deer, elk, moose, antelope
>
> Unclean: armadillo, bear, beaver, muskrat, opossum, rabbit, raccoon, squirrel, wild boar, woodchuck

Poultry/Game Birds:
> Clean: capon, chicken, cornish hen, dove, grouse, lark, partridge, pheasant, pigeon, quail, snipe, turkey
>
> Unclean: eagle, falcon, goose, osprey

Seafood:

Clean: bass, bluefish, butterfish, croker, cusk, grouper, haddock, hake, halibut, herring, kipper, mullet, pilchard, pollock, pompano, porgy, red snapper, rose fish, salmon, sea trout, shad, sole, whiting

Unclean: blue marlin, catfish, dolphin, eel, lamprey, mackerel, octopus, squid, swordfish, tuna, turbot, whale, crab, lobster, shrimp, oysters, scallops, prawn

The thought of eating some of these forbidden foods, such as dogs or cats is offensive to us, while we enjoy others regularly. Many scholars believe that these principles originated as a reflection of God's care and loving concern for his people's physical health and well-being.

If you decide to eliminate pork and shellfish from your diet, you will soon discover, as I did, that you don't even miss them. Your attitude will be the determining factor for yourself and your family. Try replacing pork and shellfish with some of the wonderfully satisfying and tasty fish, poultry, and meat dishes in this chapter.

Fish, Poultry, and Meat Tips

- Baking fish on a bed of celery and onions will add to the taste as well as keep the fish from sticking.

- Coating will adhere to chicken better if the poultry has been chilled for an hour before cooking.

- For a juicier burger, rinse both sides with cold water before grilling.

- To make gravy, fill a jar with cold water and flour, and place lid on jar tightly. Shake the jar until liquid is well mixed and lumps are gone. Then slowly add this mixture to pan drippings and stir with a wire whisk while bringing gravy to a boil.

- Always roast poultry breast side down so the white meat will not dry out. Turn the bird for the last portion of cooking so that it will brown well.

- Rubbing poultry with salt and lemon juice will reduce unpleasant odors.

- Use unwaxed dental floss for trussing poultry because it will not burn.

- If gravy is too greasy, a bit of baking soda can be added without affecting the taste.

- A dash of lemon juice and milk added to the liquid used to cook white fish will make the flesh white.

- For extra tender chicken, marinate meat in milk or buttermilk for several hours in the refrigerator before cooking.

- For easy natural juice gravy or "au jus", pour pan drippings into a tall jar. The grease will rise to the top in minutes and can be removed.

- Adding cold water to the bottom of the broiling pan before cooking meat helps absorb smoke and grease and makes cleaning up easier.

Fish cookery

How to cook: 1 (excellent); 2 (good); 3 (fair)

	Broiled	Baked	Boiled/ Steamed	Fried/ Sauteed	Months in Season
Bluefish	2	1	3		All Year
Butterfish	2	3			April-Dec
Cod	1	2			All Year
Croaker		2		1	Feb.-Nov.
Grouper			3		Nov.-April
Haddock		1			All Year
Halibut	1	2			All Year
Herring		1	2	2	All Year
Lake trout	3	1	3		April-Nov.
Mullet	1	2	3		June-Oct.
Pompano	1	2	1		All Year
Porgies	2	3			All Year
Red Snapper		1	3		All Year
Salmon		2			All Year
Sea bass		1		2	All Year
Sea trout		1	3	2	Nov.-May
Shad	2	1	1		Dec-June
Sole	2	3			All Year
Striped bass			1		All Year
Whiting					May-Dec

Cooking Instruction

Doneness	Red-Hot Charcoal 2¾" from Heat		Pre-heated Oven Broiler 2" from Heat Source	
	First Side	After Turning	First Side	After Turning
¾" Thick				
Rare	4 minutes	2 minutes	5 minutes	4 minutes
Medium	5 minutes	3 minutes	7 minutes	5 minutes
Well	7 minutes	5 minutes	10 minutes	8 minutes
1" Thick				
Rare	5 minutes	3 minutes	6 minutes	5 minutes
Medium	6 minutes	4 minutes	8 minutes	6 minutes
Well	8 minutes	6 minutes	11 minutes	9 minutes
1¼" Thick				
Rare	5 minutes	4 minutes	7 minutes	5 minutes
Medium	7 minutes	5 minutes	8 minutes	7 minutes
Well	9 minutes	7 minutes	12 minutes	10 minutes
1½" Thick				
Rare	6 minutes	4 minutes	7 minutes	6 minutes
Medium	7 minutes	6 minutes	9 minutes	7 minutes
Well	10 minutes	8 minutes	13 minutes	11 minutes
1¾" Thick				
Rare	7 minutes	5 minutes	8 minutes	7 minutes
Medium	8 minutes	7 minutes	9 minutes	8 minutes
Well	11 minutes	9 minutes	14 minutes	12 minutes

What to Serve with Fish

Trout: potato, asparagus
Baked snapper: broccoli, carrots, green salad
Broiled fillets: baked potatoes, green salad, squash, and onions
Codfish cakes: baked beans, green salad
Fillet of sole: cole slaw, black-eyed peas
Baked salmon: corn on the cob, green salad
Broiled salmon: peas, carrots
Broiled halibut: broccoli, corn on the cob

SALMON SALAD

1 (8 oz.) Salmon fillet, cooked or
  1 (6 oz.) can salmon (skinless,
  boneless), drained and flaked
½ cup sour cream
1 teaspoon yellow mustard

2 teaspoons lemon juice
1 tablespoon dill (fresh), minced
1 cup shell macaroni, cooked
2 green onions, chopped

Stir together sour cream, mustard, and lemon juice. Toss in salmon, macaroni, and onions. Serve over a bed of romaine or leaf lettuce. **Serves 2**.

SMOKED TROUT OR SALMON STUFFED EGGS

½ cup Plain yogurt
12 hard-boiled eggs, cut in
  halves with yolks removed
½ pound Smoked trout or salmon,
  skinned, boned, and flaked

1 tablespoon Lemon peel, grated
¼ cup tomato, seeded and diced
2 tablespoons fresh chives, chopped
Dash of salt and pepper

Drain yogurt over a bowl for 1 hour by pouring into a sieve lined with a paper towel. Shave a thin piece off of bottom of egg half so it will sit properly when filled. Mix together fish, lemon, tomatoes, and chives. Salt and pepper to taste. Stir in 2 to 3 tablespoons of drained yogurt until mixture is just combined. Do not over mix. Garnish with remaining chives. **Makes 24**.

Note:

*Just about any white fish can be used in the following recipes.
Experiment with some new varieties, and let your taste buds
decide which ones are best!*

BAKED FISH

1 pound fish fillets	Paprika
1 teaspoon garlic powder	1 tablespoon melted butter
1 cup whole wheat bread crumbs (fine)	Lemon wedges

Arrange fish in greased baking dish. Rub bread crumbs with palms to make
fine crumbs. Mix garlic with butter. Sprinkle bread crumbs on fish, then
drizzle butter over bread crumbs. Bake at 450° for 15 to 20 minutes or until fish
comes apart easily with a fork. Sprinkle with paprika. Serve with a lemon
wedge. **Serves 2**.

FISH PATTIES

2 pounds fish, cooked and cleaned	½ cup Bread crumbs (fine)
1 large onion, chopped	1 teaspoon tamari sauce
1 garlic clove	1 stalk celery, chopped
1 yard egg	

Saute onion, garlic, and celery in 1 tablespoon of olive oil. Add remaining
ingredients and form into patties. Brown both sides in olive oil (about 5
minutes on each side). Serve with lemon wedges. **Serves 4**.

CHOCK FULL OF CHICKEN

4 to 6 cups cooked brown rice

1 small onion, chopped

2 tablespoons butter

1 tablespoon fructose

2 tablespoons hot water

2 tablespoons slivered almonds

4 skinless, boneless chicken breasts

1 tablespoon olive oil

1⅓ cups dried cherries

¼ teaspoon ground turmeric

Salt and pepper to taste

Set aside cooked rice. In large skillet, sauté onion in olive oil until tender. Add chicken and cook until tender. Transfer chicken and onion to a bowl and set aside. In same skillet melt butter over medium heat. Press half of cooked rice in bottom of skillet. Cook, uncovered, for 5 to 8 minutes, without stirring, until rice is brown and crispy on bottom. Add remaining cooked rice, cherries, and fructose to chicken; toss to combine. Spread this over rice skillet. Dissolve turmeric in hot water. Drizzle this over rice. Top with almonds and a few cherries.

SHARON'S STYLE OF "CRUNCHY CHICKEN"

1 whole chicken or 4 breasts, both
    deboned, cooked, and chopped

4 cups cooked rice, cooked in
    defatted chicken broth

1 large onion, finely chopped

4 stalks celery, chopped

2 tablespoons minced garlic

3 teaspoon olive oil

1 cup blanched almonds

2 (12 oz.) containers cottage cheese

1 teaspoon salt

1 cup grated Cheddar cheese

1 bag baked potato chips, finely
    crushed

In skillet, sauté onion and celery in oil. Remove from heat after 5 minutes. Stir in garlic. Place cottage cheese in blender and cream until smooth (sour cream consistency). In large bowl combine chicken, rice, onions, and celery; mix well. Stir in almonds, salt and creamy cottage cheese. Spread in large oiled casserole dish. Smooth the top and sprinkle cheese evenly. Leave chips in the bag and crush. Sprinkle the crushed chips evenly over cheese. Bake at 350° for 30 minutes or until cheese is fully melted.

GRILLED CHICKEN WITH TOMATOES AND RAISIN CHUTNEY

4 to 6 boneless, skinless chicken
    breasts, cut in halves
3 medium yellow tomatoes
    peeled, seeded and chopped
1 small onion, minced
⅓ cup honey
1 teaspoon apple cider vinegar

½ teaspoon mustard
⅛ teaspoon ground allspice
½ cup golden raisins
⅛ cup water
1 tablespoon ginger root, grated
½ teaspoon ground cumin
Salt and pepper to taste

In large skillet over medium heat, combine all ingredients except chicken. Bring to a boil and simmer on low about 30 minutes, until mixture has thickened. On outdoor grill or oven broiler, grill breast about 4 inches from heat, turning until cooked thoroughly on both sides. Season with salt and pepper. Spoon chutney on grilled chicken and serve.

APRICOT-GINGER CHICKEN

4 to 6 skinless, boneless chicken
    breasts, cut in 1½ inch strips
4 cups cooked brown rice
3 tablespoons apricot jam
¾ cup crushed corn flakes

3 tablespoon chunky peanut butter
1½ cup shredded coconut
1 teaspoon ground ginger
¼ teaspoon ground cinnamon

Preheat oven to 400°. In small saucepan, stir together peanut butter and jam. Melt over low heat. Add to chicken; toss and coat. In large bowl combine coconut and corn flake crumbs, curry powder, and ginger. Put in several pieces at a time; toss and turn chicken to coat. Place chicken in large greased baking dish. Bake 8 to 10 minutes. Turn chicken and bake 8 to 10 minutes. Continue until chicken is tender and fully cooked. Mound rice in center of platter. Sprinkle with cinnamon. Arrange chicken around rice.

CINDY'S ROSEMARY CHICKEN

1 chicken, cut up or 4 chicken breasts	1 teaspoon salt
2 cloves garlic, minced	4 tablespoons dried rosemary
4 tablespoons olive oil	¼ cup Parmesan cheese, grated
½ cup fine bread crumbs	

Preheat oven to 375°. In small bowl combine oil, garlic, salt, and 2 tablespoons dried rosemary. In another small bowl combine bread crumbs and parmesan cheese. Take each piece of chicken and roll in oil, and garlic, then roll same piece of chicken in bread crumbs. Place chicken in oiled baking dish, breaded side up. Cover with foil and bake for 50 minutes. Uncover and bake 20 to 30 minutes or until chicken is thoroughly cooked. **Serves 4**.

LEMON CHICKEN

4 large chicken breasts (skinned and boned)	1 lemon, thinly sliced
¼ teaspoon pepper	1 teaspoon salt
2 tablespoons butter	½ cup unbleached flour
¼ cup dry cooking wine	1 tablespoon olive oil
1 tablespoon butter	¼ cup fresh lemon juice
	2 tablespoons fresh parsley, minced

Mix together salt, pepper, and flour. Dip chicken in flour and shake off excess. Set aside. In large skillet, melt butter and oil over medium heat. Saute chicken until lightly brown, about 3 minutes per side. Remove from skillet and place on paper towels, turning once to absorb excess oils. Combine wine and lemon juice; pour into skillet. Bring to a boil, scraping any chicken bits into center of skillet. Add chicken and simmer for 5 minutes. Remove chicken to heated platter. Bring liquid in skillet to a boil. Reduce liquid to 2 tablespoons, then stir in butter. Pour over chicken. Garnish with parsley and lemon slices.

CHICKEN ENCHILADAS

1 whole chicken, boiled, deboned, and
  torn into small pieces
1 large jar tomato or spaghetti sauce
  (reserve ½ cup For top of enchiladas)
2 medium onions
1 large bunch cilantro

1 teaspoon oregano
1 pkg. whole wheat flour tortillas
1 medium green pepper
1 tablespoon garlic (minced, jar)
¼ teaspoon salt
½ cup grated white Cheddar cheese

In large skillet, sauté onions and pepper for 5 to 10 minutes. Add remaining ingredients. Cover and simmer for 15 minutes. Turn off heat. Spray a 15-by-10-inch oblong casserole dish with cooking spray. Place 1 tortilla in your hand; add 2 heaping tablespoons of chicken mixture in center of the tortilla. Roll up the tortilla and place in the oiled casserole dish. Repeat with remaining tortillas until you have enchiladas laying in a row form end to end. Spread reserved ½ cup of tomato sauce evenly over all enchiladas. Sprinkle cheese down center of rows. Bake at 350° for 20 minutes. Serve with favorite salsa. **Serves 6 to 8**.

CHICKEN AND RICE CREAM CASSEROLE

2 to 3 cups chopped chicken
4 cups cooked brown or basmati rice
1 medium onion, chopped
1 (16 ounce) package french style
  green beans, thawed
1 (8 ounce) can water chestnuts,
  sliced and drained

1 (8 ounce) can cream of celery soup
1 (8 ounce) sour cream
⅛ teaspoon salt
½ cup Swiss cheese, shredded

Mix all ingredients together except cheese. Place in large oiled casserole dish. Top with cheese. Bake at 350° for 30 minutes. **Serves 6**.

BAKED-FRIED CHICKEN

1 whole chicken, skinned and cut
3 eggs beaten
2 cups crushed Corn Flakes or
    favorite flakes
½ cup flour

½ teaspoon salt
½ teaspoon pepper
¼ teaspoon Stevia or
    1 tablespoon fructose
Olive oil

In a large bowl, mix Corn Flakes, flour, salt, pepper and Stevia to make dry mixture. Dip each piece of chicken into beaten eggs. Press chicken into dry mixture to coat it. Place each piece of chicken top side down into skillet with enough olive oil to cover bottom of pan. Cook each piece for about 30 seconds. Place chicken top side up in large oiled casserole dish. Top with salt and pepper. Cover and bake at 350° for 30 minutes. Uncover and cook until Corn Flakes start to lighty brown.

What to Serve with Meats

Roast Turkey: carrots, sweet potatoes, string beans casserole, wild rice, greens
Roast Beef: barley soup, peas and carrots, vegetable soup, rice, spinach, broccoli
Stuffed Cabbage: rye bread, asparagus
Pepper Steak: baked potatoes, peas, tossed salad, squash
Veal Cutlet: baked potato, tossed salad
Lamb Chops: carrots, parsley, potatoes, spinach, peas
Lamb Stew: dumplings, green salad
Roast Lamb: mashed potatoes, currant jelly
Hamburger: potato salad, carrots, baked potatoes
Corned Beef Hash: poached eggs, green salad
Meatloaf: baked potato, green salad, peas
Chipped Beef: baked potato, green salad, peas

To Prepare Your Steaks

Thaw in refrigerator; bring meat to room temperature before cooking. You can successfully cook frozen steaks. Start by searing both sides to seal in juices. Then reduce heat for slow cooking to allow the inside to thaw. Follow the following chart, but allow about twice the cooking time for frozen steaks.

For juicier and more flavorful steaks, tongs should be used when handling or turning. Cooking units vary of course, and it is always advisable to run your own tests when cooking steaks. Use the following chart as a guide.

The following cooking times are for fully thawed steaks.

Filet mignons take one to two minutes less total time to cook.

If you prefer to cook your steaks in your conventional oven, do not thaw, and preheat over to 450°. As a guide for medium-rare steaks allow approximately

- 10-11 minutes per side for an 8 ounce filet of prime rib
- 12-13 minutes per side for an 8 ounce top sirloin
- 9 minutes per side for an 11 or 12 ounce boneless strip sirloin
- 10-11 minutes per side for a 6 ounce filet mignon

Because ovens may vary in the amount of heat produced and the best distance to place the meat from the burners, tests on your equipment are valuable.

Meat Preparation Chart

Roasting

Cut		Weight	Cooking Range Temp.	Internal Heat Temp.	Approximate Time
Beef	Standing Ribs (3)	6-8 lbs.	325°F		
	Rare			140°F	16-18 min. / lb.
	Medium			160°F	20-22 min. / lb.
	Well Done			170°F	25-30 min. / lb.
	Rolled Rib	5-7 lbs.	325°F		Add 10-12 min. / lb. to above time
	Rump Boneless	5-7 lbs.	325°F	170°F	30 min. / lb.
Veal	Leg (center cut)	7-8 lbs.	325°F	170°F	25 min. / lb.
	Loin	4½-5 lbs.	325°F	170°F	30-35 min. / lb.
	Rack 4-6 ribs	2½ -3 lbs.	325°F	170°F	30-35 min. / lb.
	Shoulder Bone-in	6-7 lbs.	325°F	170°F	25 min. / lb.
	Shoulder Boneless Roll	5-6 lbs.	325°F	170°F	35-40 min. / lb.
Lamb	Leg	6-7 lbs.	325°F	175-180°F	30-35 min. / lb.
	Shoulder Bone-in	5-7 lbs.	325°F	175-180°F	30-35 min. / lb.
	Shoulder Boneless Roll	4-6 lbs.	325°F	175-180°F	40-45 min. / lb.
Chicken	Stuff Weight	4-5 lbs.	325°F	185°F	35-40 min. / lb.
	Chicken	over 5 lbs.	325°F	185°F	20-25 min. / lb.
Turkey	Stuff Weight	6-10 lbs.	325°F	185°F	20-25 min. / lb.
	Turkey	10-16 lbs.	325°F	185°F	18-20 min. / lb.
	Turkey	18-25 lbs.	325°F	185°F	15-18 min. / lb.

Geese — same as turkey of similar weight.
Duck — same as heavy chicken of similar weight.

Broiling

Cut		Thickness	Weight	Approximate Total Time (min.)		
				Rare	Medium	Well Done
Beef	Rib Steak	1 inch	1½ lbs.	8-10	12-14	18-20
	Club Steak	1 inch	1½ lbs.	8-10	12-14	18-20
	Porterhouse	1 inch	1½ lbs.	10-12	14-16	20-25
		1½ inch	2½-3 lbs.	14-16	18-20	25-30
		2 inch	3-3½ lbs.	20-25	30-35	40-45
	Sirloin	1 inch	2½ - 3½ lbs.	10-12	14-16	20-25
		1½ inch	3½ - 4½ lbs.	14-16	18-20	25-30
		2 inch	5-5½ lbs.	20-25	30-35	40-45
	Ground Beef Patties	¾ inch	4 oz. ea.	8	12	15
	Tenderloin	1 inch		8-10	12-14	18-20
Lamb	**Rib or Loin**					
	Chops (1 rib)	¾ inch	2-3 oz. ea.			14-15
	Double Rib	1½ inch	4-5 oz. ea.			22-25
	Lamb Shoulder					
	Chops	¾ inch	3-4 oz. ea.			14-15
		1½ inch	5-6 oz. ea.			22-25
	Lamb Patties	¾ inch	4 oz. ea.			14-15

Braising

Cut		Weight	Approximate Time
Beef	Beef Pot Roast, Chuck Rump or Heel of Round	3-5 lbs.	Brown then simmer 3½ - 4 hours
	Swiss Steak (round) 1 inch thick	2 lbs.	Brown then simmer 1½ - 2 hours
	Flank Steak	1½ -2 lbs.	Brown then simmer 1½ hours
	Beef Short Ribs	2-2½ lbs.	Brown then simmer 2- 2½ hours
Lamb	Rolled Lamb Shoulder Pot Roast	3-5 lbs.	Brown then simmer 2- 2½ hours
	Lamb Shoulder Chops	4-5 oz. ea.	Brown then simmer 35-40 min.
	Lamb Neck Slices	½ lb. ea.	Brown then simmer 1- 1½ hours.
	Lamb Shanks	1 lb. ea.	Brown then simmer 1½ hours
	Veal Rolled Shoulder Pot Roast	4-5½ lbs.	Brown then simmer 2- 2½ hours
	Cutlets or Round	2 lbs.	Brown then simmer 45-50 min.
	Loin or Rib Chops	3-5 oz. ea.	Brown then simmer 45-50 min.

Stewing

Cut	Weight	Approximate Time
Beef – 1- 1½ inch cubes from neck, chuck plate or heel of round	2 lbs.	2½ - 3 hours
Veal or Lamb 1- 1½ inch cubes from shoulder or breast	2 lbs.	1½ - 2 hours
Chicken	3½ - 4 lbs.	2- 2½ hours

Simmering in water

Cut	Weight	Approximate Time
Fresh Beef Brisket or Plate	8 lbs.	4-5 hours total
Corned Beef Brisket half or whole	4-8 lbs.	4-6 hours total
Cross Cut Shanks of Beef	4 lbs.	3-4 hours total

MOM'S HOMEMADE TACOS

1 pound Lean ground beef, browned
1 can refried beans (Bearito brand)
1 can jalapeno bean dip

Dash of salt
10 to 12 corn tortillas

After browning beef, add refried beans. Mix well, then add bean dip. Mix well again. Heat up slowly on low heat. Cover and turn off heat so that taco meat won't dry out. Take tortilla and steam one at a time.

Toppings:

Chopped leaf lettuce
Chopped tomatoes
Sour Cream (you can substitute this by
        placing organic cottage cheese
        in a blender until creamy)

Grated Cheddar cheese
Picante sauce

This is a fun meal, but a little messy. Place beef mixture, steamed tortillas, and favorite toppings on the table. Fill tortillas half full with beef mixture, then add toppings. **Serves 5 to 6**.

MOIST MEATLOAF

1 pound lean ground beef

1 egg, beaten

1 slice whole wheat bread (crumbs)

1 finely chopped onion

¼ cup finely chopped tomato

⅛ teaspoon salt

1 tablespoon chopped or crushed garlic

2 cups Pasta sauce

Mix together all ingredients. Form into a loaf shape and place in a loaf pan. Be careful that loaf is not too thick so that it will cook thoroughly. Bake at 350° for 30 minutes or until done in the middle. Spread pasta sauce on top. Place back in oven for 10 to 15 minutes. **Serves 4**.

BEST BURGERS

1 pound Lean ground beef

1 egg, beaten

⅛ teaspoon salt

1 teaspoon fresh minced garlic

¼ cup finely chopped onion

2 tablespoon Worcestershire sauce

Mix all ingredients thoroughly. Form into ½ inch patties. Brown until done all the way through. Serve with your favorite condiments on whole wheat buns.

Can also be served as salisbury steak or topped with sautéed onions.

VEGGIE AND BEEF TACO SALAD

1 pound cooked ground beef
1 large onion, chopped
1 tablespoon olive oil
1 large tomato, diced
1 cup water
1 tablespoon sorghum
2 heads leaf lettuce, torn
½ cup grated Cheddar cheese

1 teaspoon salt
1 tablespoon chili powder*
1 medium red bell pepper
1 can kidney beans
2 tablespoons cornmeal
2 tomatoes, chopped
1 teaspoon garlic

In large skillet sauté onion in oil. Add bell pepper and tomato. Cook on low for 10 minutes. In small bowl, mix together water, fructose, salt, cornmeal, and garlic powder. Pour over vegetables and stir.

Stir in ground beef, beans, chili powder. Simmer for 5 minutes. Refrigerate 1 hour. In large salad bowl chop up lettuce and tomato. Stir in chilled taco mixture. Top with grated cheese. Serve chilled. **Serves 8**.

* Start out by adding 1 tablespoon of chili powder. Add more depending on how spicy you like your food.

Beans, Lentils *and* Rice

Main Dishes
Side Dishes

5

Beans, Lentils and Rice

Beans are delicious, though often unappreciated marvels. They top the charts for versatility and are amazingly high in protein, making them an excellent dietary staple for vegetarians and non-vegetarians alike. Beans, lentils, and rice offer a very inexpensive way to build good nutrition into your family's diet. Begin using these terrific foods more often — you may see your weekly grocery bill start to shrink!

Beans and Lentils — Variety Is the Key

How many of the legumes (beans) listed have you eaten regularly? How many have your tried? Which ones have you never tried? Why not select one or two new varieties to pick up at your grocers this week? Go ahead and experiment. Discover what a wonderful treat you've been missing!

Aduki beans	Lentils
Black beans	Lima beans
Black-eyed peas	Navy beans
English peas	Pinto beans
Garbanzo beans	Soybeans
Great Northern beans	Sugar peas
Green beans	Wax beans
Kidney beans	

Cooking Beans and Lentils

Be sure to wash your beans and lentils, and pick out any tiny stones or other matter. Drain beans and soak them in distilled water. Lentils and split peas do not need to be soaked since they cook more quickly than beans.

Quick Soaking Method

After beans have been washed and drained, cover them with boiling water and allow them to soak for at least 2 hours.

Overnight Soaking Method

I have found that the easiest and quickest way of cooking beans is to soak them first. I find it very convenient to soak them overnight and simmer them while preparing the meal. Soak at least 6 to 8 hours or overnight. Be sure the beans are covered with a couple inches of water since they will swell.

Brown Rice

Brown rice is a high protein grain with 8 vitamins. It is best purchased as "organic brown rice". The natural bran layer of brown rice remains intact, and organic varieties have not been sprayed with chemicals.

Try preparing brown rice mixed with wild rice. They complement each other very nicely. Wild rice is expensive, so I always mix 3 parts of brown rice to 1 part of wild rice. Wild rice has a nutty flavor and is very tasty.

Cooking Brown Rice

Always rinse rice thoroughly before cooking. It is best to serve brown rice immediately. You'll be delighted to find that brown rice does not get sticky and clump together as white rice tends to do.

Cooking Dried Beans, Lentils and Rice

One Cup	Water	Cook	Yield
Black Beans	4 cups	1½ hours	2 cups
Black-eyed Peas	3 cups	1½ hours	2 cups
Garbanzo Beans	4 cups	3 hours	2 cups
Great Northern	3 cups	2 hours	2 cups
Kidney Beans	3 cups	1½ hours	2 cups
Lima Beans	2 cups	1½ hours	1½ cups
Pinto Beans	3 cups	2½ hours	2 cups
Navy Beans	2 cups	1½ hours	2 cups
Soybeans	3 cups	3 hours	2 cups
Lentils	3 cups	1 hours	2½ cups
Brown Rice	2 cups	1 hours	3 cups
Wild Rice	3 cups	1½ hours	4 cups

BASIL GREEN BEANS

1 pound Cut green beans (or frozen)	2 tablespoon Raw butter
1 clove garlic, minced	1 teaspoon Dried basil

Cut green beans into 1 inch pieces. Cook in water just covering beans. Cover and simmer for 15 to 20 minutes. In small skillet sauté garlic in butter. Drain beans and add butter, garlic, and basil. Mix well and serve. **Serves 6**.

DILLED GREEN BEANS

½ cup water	½ teaspoon dill weed
1 pound cut green beans	½ teaspoon thyme
1 medium onion	1 teaspoon salt

Bring water to a boil, reduce heat, and add all ingredients. Cook on low for 30 minutes or until beans are tender. **Serves 6**.

GREEN BEANS ALMONDINE

4 cup green beans (fresh or frozen)	½ cup chopped almond
2 tablespoons butter	1 teaspoon lemon (freshly squeezed
¼ cup water	1 tablespoon tamari sauce

Saute beans in butter in skillet. Gradually add water and simmer for 15 minutes. Stir in tamari sauce and cook for 5 more minutes. Add lemon juice and almonds; serve. **Serves 4 to 6**.

Spanish Lima Beans

3 cups lima beans (fresh or frozen)
1½ cup dried lima beans
3 cups water
1 large onion, chopped
1 clove garlic, minced
2 tablespoons olive oil

1 cup tomato, chopped
½ cup celery, chopped
1 tablespoon tamari sauce
½ teaspoon worcestershire sauce
½ cup grated Cheddar cheese

If using dried beans, cook for about 1½ hours. Cook for 20 minutes if beans are fresh. After beans are done, drain water. In large skillet, sauté onion and celery. Add tomato and simmer for 15 minutes. Stir in beans and sauces. Grease 2 quart baking dish and pour in bean mixture. Lightly stir in cheese. Bake at 350° for 30 minutes. **Serves 6**.

Kidney Beans Side Dish

3 cups water or leftover vegetable broth
1¼ cups dried kidney beans
1 medium green pepper, chopped
1 medium tomato, chopped

1 clove garlic, minced
1 large onion, chopped
½ teaspoon olive oil
1 tablespoon chili powder

Cook beans for 1 hour, covered. Add remaining ingredients and cook for 30 minutes more. Serve. **Serves 4**.

Wild Rice Pilaf

3½ cups chicken broth

1 cup natural brown rice

½ cup wild rice

1 clove garlic, minced

1 onion, chopped

2 stalks celery, chopped

⅓ cup chopped almonds

1 tablespoon tamari sauce

2 tablespoon fresh parsley, chopped

1 cup frozen peas

¼ teaspoon sea salt

In large sauce pan, add broth and bring to a boil. Add all ingredients except almonds and peas. Brown almonds in 2 tablespoons butter. Cook rice for 40 minutes. Add almonds and peas. Cook 20 minutes, then serve. **Serves 6**.

Southern Baked Beans

2 cups dried navy beans (or 4 cans organic pinto beans)

4 cups water

2 onions, chopped

½ teaspoon mustard

¼ teaspoon worcestershire sauce

1 cup tomato sauce

¼ cup fructose

1 clove garlic, minced

Cook beans in water for about 2 hours. Drain water and save. In large baking dish, mix beans and remaining ingredients with 1 cup of bean water. Cover and bake at 350° for 2 hours. Serve hot or cold. (Quick way: Replace dried beans and water with 3 to 4 cans of organic baked beans.)

Old-Fashioned Black-Eyed Peas

3 cups water

1 cup dried black-eyed peas (or 2 cans organic black-eyed peas)

1 large onion, chopped

1 pinch of cayenne pepper

1 clove garlic, minced

1 medium tomato, chopped

1 tablespoon tamari sauce

Cook peas in water and seasoning for 30 minutes. Add remaining ingredients and cook, covered, for 30 more minutes. **Serves 6**.

SPANISH RICE

2 tablespoons olive oil

1 onion, chopped

1 cup water

½ cup chopped celery

1 teaspoon garlic powder

1 tablespoon curry powder

1 cup tomato sauce

1 cup picante sauce

1 teaspoon mustard

1 tablespoon tamari sauce

2½ cups cooked brown rice

In large skillet, sauté onion in oil. Add sauces, then add remaining ingredients. Stir in cooked rice. Simmer 15 minutes. **Serves 4**.

BLACK BEANS AND RICE

3 cups cooked black beans

1 cup onion, chopped

1 clove garlic, minced

2 tablespoon olive oil

1 cup green pepper, chopped

1 large tomato, chopped

1 tablespoon tamari sauce

2 teaspoons cumin

⅛ teaspoon cayenne pepper

½ cup picante sauce

In large skillet, sauté onion and garlic for 2 minutes. Add green pepper and sauté for 2 more minutes. Add remaining ingredients except picante sauce; cover and simmer for 20 minutes. Gradually add picante sauce as needed. Serve over cooked brown rice. **Serves 4**.

CONFETTI RICE

1 tablespoon butter	1 medium onion, chopped
1 can chicken broth	¾ cup brown or basmati rice
1 carrot, finely sliced	1 yellow squash, cubed
1 cup fresh broccoli tops	½ teaspoon Dried basil
½ cup Parmesan cheese (shredded)	

In large saucepan, sauté onion in butter over medium heat until tender. Add chicken broth and rice; bring to a boil. Add basil. Cover and simmer on low for 15 minutes. Place vegetables on top of rice. Cover and cook for another 10 to 15 minutes or until rice and vegetables are tender. Top with cheese. **Serves 4**

RICE PILAF

2½ cups chicken broth	1 small cinnamon stick
¼ cup chopped chicken	2 tablespoons olive oil
¼ cup pine nuts	1½ cups brown rice
1 medium onion, finely chopped	¼ cup golden raisins, moistened.

Heat chicken broth in saucepan. In large skillet, gently sauté almonds and pine nuts in olive oil until slightly brown. Do not burn. Remove nuts from oil. Stir onion in oil and sauté for about 10 minutes. Stir in rice and continue cooking and stirring for about 5 minutes. Pour heated broth in with rice. Stir rice and cook over low heat for about 20 minutes, until all liquid is absorbed. Remove from heat, cover, and let set for 5 minutes. Remove cinnamon stick and stir in raisins.

SPICE RICE PILAF

1 cup brown rice	1 small onion, chopped
1 tablespoon olive oil	¼ teaspoon ground coriander
¼ teaspoon ground cinnamon	½ teaspoon ground cardomon
¼ teaspoon ground cumin	⅛ teaspoon ground nutmeg
½ cup water	1 cup chopped spinach, water
1⅓ cups chicken or vegetable broth	squeezed out
¼ cup golden raisins	¼ cup sliced almonds

In skillet, cook onion in oil until tender. Stir in brown rice and all ground spices. Cook over medium heat about 5 to 10 minutes or until rice is a golden brown. Add broth and water. Bring to a boil; reduce heat. Cover and simmer until rice is tender. Remove from heat and let stand, covered, for 10 minutes. Stir in spinach, almonds, and raisins. **Serves 4 to 6**.

RICE BROCCOLI CASSEROLE

5 cups cooked brown rice	½ cup grated Cheddar cheese
2 cups steamed broccoli	1 cup whole wheat bread crumbs
1 large onion, chopped	2 teaspoons garlic powder
2 tablespoons olive oil	¼ teaspoon cayenne pepper
2 eggs	1 tablespoon coriander
1 cup raw yogurt	¼ teaspoon sea salt
1 tablespoon tamari	

Saute onion in oil. Mix together eggs, yogurt, and tamari sauce. Stir in cheese and bread crumbs. Mix in remaining ingredients. Place in casserole dish and bake at 350° for 30 minutes. **Serves 6**.

LENTILS AND RICE

3 cups water	1 tablespoon tamari sauce
1 cup lentils	2 tablespoons fresh parsley, chopped
1 onion, chopped	¼ teaspoon sea salt
1 clove garlic, minced	½ teaspoon curry powder

In saucepan, bring water to a boil. Add all ingredients and cook on low for 1 hour. Serve over rice.

1 cup brown rice	1 onion, chopped
2 cup water	1 tablespoon tamari sauce

In saucepan, bring water to a boil. Add all ingredients and cook on low for 1 hour. **Serves 4**.

LENTIL BURGERS

1 cup lentils, washed and drained	1 clove garlic, minced
3 cups water	½ cup carrot, grated
1 onion, minced	1 egg
¾ cup whole wheat flour	2 tablespoon tamari sauce
½ teaspoon marjoram	½ teaspoon thyme

In saucepan, bring water to a boil. Reduce heat and add lentils, garlic, and tamari sauce. Cook on low for 1 hour. Beat egg and mix with flour. Add remaining ingredients to flour and mix thoroughly. Stir in lentils and mix well. Form into burger patties. Cook in skillet in small amount of olive oil. Brown on each side. **Serves 4**.

RICE TOSSED SALAD

1 head leaf lettuce	2 scallions, diced
3 cups spinach, torn	1 medium green pepper
½ cup carrots, grated	1 cup cooked brown rice

Tear lettuce and mix with spinach. Add remaining ingredients. Toss and mix in dressing. Top with 2 tablespoons Parmesan cheese (optional). **Serves 6.**

HERB DRESSING

¼ cup vinegar	¼ teaspoon Oregano
¼ cup olive oil	¼ teaspoon Dried parsley
1 clove garlic, minced	¼ teaspoon Garlic powder
¼ teaspoon Basil	1 tablespoon Sorghum

Mix together ingredients. It is best to store in refrigerator for several hours before using.

BEAN ENCHILADAS

2 large onions, chopped	1 teaspoon garlic powder
½ teaspoon salt (optional)	1 cup raw cheese, grated
6 cups cooked pinto beans	12 to 14 frozen corn taco
1 can jalapeno bean dip (Hains	shells, thawed
brand is good)	Mild or hot taco sauce

In large skillet, sauté onions. Take out 1 cup and set aside . Mash beans and add them and bean dip to onions. Keep on low heat. Add garlic, salt, and ½ cup of cheese. Mix well.

Fill taco shells with bean mixture (2 to 3 tablespoons). Roll up shell and place in large glass baking dish. Repeat until bean mixture is used up. Spread 1 cup sautéed onions over enchiladas, then sprinkle remaining cheese over onions. Cover and bake at 350° for 30 minutes. Serve with taco sauce. Excellent when served with rice and salad. **Serves 4 to 6**.

NOTES

Savory
Soups *and*
Sandwiches

Hot Soups
Chilled Soups
Fruit Soups
Sandwiches

6

Savory Soups and Sandwiches

What could be more delicious on a chilly winter's day (and summer days too) than a hearty bowl of homemade soup? I love making soups for my family. I start the soup pot simmering in the morning, and by dinner we have a wonderfully tasty meal — and with very little effort!

There are so many reasons for making homemade soups. They provide a simple way to get much-needed vitamins, minerals and enzymes into my family's diet, and they are so convenient. I usually make twice as much as we will use and freeze the rest for later. If you have a baby, soups can be prepared easily in a baby food grinder for your tiniest family member.

If you work outside the home, a crock pot of homemade soup will welcome your weary family back home with a delicious, ready meal. And with an inexpensive breadmaker, you can even come home to homemade bread and soup. What a treat! In our house, we all love the comforting aroma of homemade soup cooking in the kitchen.

Helpful Hints in the Kitchen
(The Soup Pot)

- Steak, roast, or poultry bones can be frozen until needed for soup stock.
- If the soup or stew is too salty, add cut raw potatoes. Discard them once they have cooked and have absorbed the salt.
- To prevent curdling of the milk or cream in soup, add the soup to the milk rather than vice versa. Or, add a bit of flour to the milk and beat well before combining.
- Always start cooking bones and meat in cold water.
- The easiest way to skim off fat from soup is to chill until the fat hardens on top of the liquid. If time will not permit this, wrap ice in paper toweling and skim over the top.
- To add great flavor to soup after serving, have a bottle of Balanced Mineral Bouillon on the table (see appendix).

MISO SOUP

8 cups water or soup stock	1 cup shredded cabbage
2 carrots, shredded	1 tablespoon miso
1 onion, chopped	1 scallion, sliced

Bring water or broth to a boil and add vegetables. Cover and cook on low for 30 minutes. Add miso after vegetables are cooked and simmer for 5 minutes. Garnish with chopped scallions.

Cooking with Miso

Miso is a fermented paste puree made from aged soybeans, and it can be found in health food store. Miso contains live enzymes and minerals, which aid in proper body metabolism and digestion. It is excellent for individuals on a low cholesterol diet. The soybeans in miso break down to about 34 percent protein, 18 percent fat, and 31 percent carbohydrates. Miso also contains lecithin and linoleic acid. Lecithin is needed by every living cell in the body.

Guideline for Using Miso in Soup

Because of the extra nutrition it provides, in addition to other tremendous qualities such as cancer-fighting properties, I try to use miso in as many of my soups as possible. Here are some helpful tips for using miso:

1. Since miso contains live enzymes, it should never be boiled.

2. Start with a cup of cooked broth from your soup. Use 1 tablespoon of miso (if you or your family has never tasted it before) mixed with the cup of broth. Stir well, or puree until creamy. Pour this back into soup pot. Stir until thoroughly mixed in with soup. Cover and let steep for 5 minutes.

3. Miso also has a salty flavor, so it's best not to add salt until you have tasted the soup with miso.

LENTIL MISO SOUP

8 cups water or leftover vegetable broth	1 stalk celery, chopped
1½ cups lentils	2 tablespoons fresh parsley, chopped
3 onions, chopped	1 clove garlic, minced
2 carrots, grated	2 tablespoons barley miso

Cook on all ingredients in crock pot (except miso) for 6 to 8 hours, or cook on stove for 3 hours. At the end of cooking time, take 1 cup of broth and mix together with miso until smooth. Add miso to soup and simmer for 1 minute. **Serves 8 to 10**.

SPLIT PEA SOUP

6 cups water or chicken broth	1 tablespoon butter
2 cups washed split peas	1½ cup chopped tomatoes
½ cup brown rice	½ cup grated carrots
½ tablespoon garlic powder	1 teaspoon salt
1 teaspoon cumin	

Bring water or broth to a boil. Add all ingredients and simmer for 2 hours or until peas are tender. For a thinner soup, add a little more water after soup has cooked for 1 hour. Season to taste at dinner table. **Serves 6**.

BLACK BEAN SOUP

5 cups water or leftover vegetable broth
1 bag black beans, washed and drained
2 onions, chopped
1 tablespoon olive oil
1 stalk celery, chopped
¼ teaspoon sea salt
½ teaspoon basil

1 carrot, grated
¼ cup fresh cilantro, chopped
1 cup natural tomato sauce
2 tablespoons tamari sauce
2 tablespoons fresh lemon juice
1 clove garlic, minced

In large saucepan bring water to a boil. Add beans and oil; simmer for 2 hours. Add remaining ingredients, except lemon juice and cilantro, and simmer for 30 minutes. Add cilantro and simmer for 15 minutes. Add lemon juice and stir well. **Serves 6**.

CHICKEN NOODLE SOUP

1 whole chicken, washed and cut up
2 quarts water
2 cups carrots, grated
1 bag frozen peas

1 (8 to 10 oz.) package artichoke or
    whole wheat noodles
½ teaspoon basil
⅛ teaspoon sea salt
1 large onion, chopped

Place chicken in water and bring to a boil. Cover and simmer for 2 hours. Debone chicken and strain broth. Refrigerate to harden fat, and skim fat off top. Place vegetables in broth and simmer for 15 minutes. Add noodles and simmer for 10 to 12 minutes. Add chicken. Salt to taste. **Serves 6**.

CHICKEN AND RICE SOUP

Use chicken noodle recipe. Replace 1 cup of brown rice for the noodles. Pour rice in with the vegetables and cook for 1 hour instead of 45 minutes.

ALPHABET SOUP

3 cans chicken broth

3 cups water

1 carrot, grated

1 clove garlic, minced

3 tomatoes, chopped

1 large onion, chopped

1 cup corn (fresh)

1 can lima beans

½ cup whole wheat alphabet noodles

1 stalk celery, chopped

Combine all ingredients except noodles. Simmer for 30 minutes. Add noodles and simmer for 15 more minutes. **Serves 8**.

BEST CHILI

1 pound dark ground turkey (or lean ground beef)*

½ cup brown rice

2 cups chicken broth

4 cups cooked kidney beans

1 large onion, chopped

2 cups cut corn

5 cups water

1 bunch cilantro, chopped

1 large tomato, chopped

2 tablespoons chili powder

1 tablespoon cumin

½ teaspoon cayenne pepper (optional for spicier chili)

3 tablespoons fructose

1 large bell pepper, chopped

In skillet brown meat. In large 4½ quart or larger pot combine water, chicken broth, and rice. Bring to a boil. Simmer for 20 minutes. Add remaining ingredients and beef. Simmer for 30 minutes. This is great served with hot corn bread (see chapter four).

*Dark turkey looks more like hamburger than white ground turkey.

POTATO SOUP

4 cup water or broth	1 tablespoon corn starch
2 cup diced potatoes	1 tablespoon butter
1 large onion, chopped	⅛ teaspoon sea salt
1 cup celery, chopped	1 teaspoon tamari sauce
1 cup milk	

Combine vegetables with water. Bring to a boil. Simmer for 45 minutes. Mix together milk, corn starch, and tamari sauce until smooth. Add this to soup. Simmer 10 minutes. Stir in butter. **Serves 4**.

TORTILLA SOUP

1 pound cooked diced chicken	1 cup water
1 cubanelle pepper, finely chopped	½ teaspoon chili powder
1 poblano pepper, finely chopped	½ teaspoon salt
1 large onion, chopped	1 teaspoon cumin
1 (16 oz.) can diced tomatoes	½ cup fresh chopped cilantro
1 (8 oz.) can tomato puree	Tortilla chips (broken up)
2 cups defatted chicken broth	½ cup grated Cheddar cheese

In large soup pot combine first 11 ingredients. Simmer for 20 minutes. Add cilantro and simmer for 10 minutes. Sprinkle chips over each serving, then add grated cheese.

BULGUR CHILI

6 cups water

1 cup chicken broth

2 large onion, chopped

2 large cloves minced garlic

1 large green pepper, chopped

1 large tomato, chopped

¼ cup bulgur

2 tablespoons chili powder

¼ cup fructose

1 tablespoon cumin

2 tablespoons fresh parsley, chopped

4 cups cooked kidney beans

1 cup cut corn

1 ½ cups plain tomato sauce

½ teaspoon sea salt

In large cooking pot, combine water and chicken broth. In skillet, sauté garlic, onion, and green pepper in a little oil. Cook until tender. Add to water, sautéed vegetables, and remaining ingredients except beans. Simmer, covered, for 1 hour. Stir occasionally. Stir in beans and simmer for 15 minutes. **Serves 10**.

CREAM OF BROCCOLI SOUP

3 cups milk

1 cup water

2 tablespoons butter

2 tablespoons corn starch

2 cups cheese, grated

1 large head broccoli, chopped

1 large onion, chopped

1 cup carrots, grated

1 tablespoon tamari sauce

Dash of rosemary (ground)

1 teaspoon salt (optional)

In 2 quart pot, add water, broccoli, onion, carrots, and rosemary. Bring water to a boil. Cover and simmer for 15 minutes. Set aside off burner. In saucepan, melt butter and gradually stir in corn starch. When lumps have dissolved, add milk and stir briskly with a fork. When mixture thickens, add cheese until creamy. Pour this in slowly with vegetables. Stir until water is mixed in with milk mixture. Add tamari sauce and simmer for 5 minutes. **Serves 4**.

ONION SOUP

6 cups water or broth

6 large onions, thinly sliced

2 tablespoons tamari sauce

1 tablespoon fructose

2 tablespoons Parmesan cheese, grated

2 tablespoons olive oil

Croutons

Saute onions lightly in olive oil. Add all ingredients to water (except cheese and croutons). Simmer for 30 minutes. Spoon croutons on top of each bowl of soup. Sprinkle cheese on top. **Serves 6**.

YOGURT-CUCUMBER SOUP

5 medium seeded cucumbers, peeled and coarsely chopped

½ cup chopped green onion (including green tops)

2 tablespoons fresh dill (or fresh mint)

¼ cup freshly squeezed lemon juice

1 cup chicken or vegetable broth

4 cup plain low fat yogurt

Puree in blender or food processor: Cucumber, onion, dill, lemon juice, and broth. Add yogurt until smooth. Season to taste with salt and pepper. Pour into tightly covered containers and chill for at least 2 hours. Garnish with fresh dill, mint, and/or carrot curls.

COCONUT-BANANA SOUP

4 cups non-fat milk

1 cup unsweetened dried coconut

4 cups ripe but firm bananas

2 tablespoons fresh ginger root minced

⅛ teaspoon ground cinnamon

1 tablespoon freshly squeezed lemon juice

Toasted, shredded coconut for garnish

In large saucepan, bring to a boil milk and coconut. Cover and let stand for 20 minutes. Add bananas, ginger, half of cinnamon, and lemon juice. Cover and cook on low about 10 minutes. Allow soup to completely cool. Transfer to a food processor or blender. Puree until smooth. Chill in refrigerator at least 1 hour. Garnish with toasted coconut.

FRUIT SOUP

1½ cups peaches, sliced

1 cup apricots, pitted and sliced

1 cup blueberries

⅛ cup fructose

2½ cups apples, sliced

1 cup plums, pitted and halved

1 cup cherries (pitted) or seedless
grapes

½ cup freshly squeezed lemon juice

4 cups water

Topping:

1 (8 oz.) container vanilla yogurt

⅛ teaspoon cinnamon

Slices of fresh fruit or berries

In large saucepan, combine fruit, fructose, ¼ cup lemon juice, and water; bring to a boil. Reduce heat and simmer for about 15 minutes. In food processor or blender puree until fairly smooth. Blend in remaining lemon juice. Pour into dish and refrigerate, uncovered, until cooled. Tightly cover and chill for 2 hours. Garnish with spoonful of yogurt, cinnamon and fruit.

Helpful Hints in the Kitchen

The Salad Bowl

- To remove the core from a head of lettuce, hit the core end sharply against the countertop or side of sink. Then the core will twist out easily.

- For cool, crisp salads, place salad greens or cole slaw in a metal bowl and place in the freezer for a few minutes.

- Rubbing waxed paper over the inside and outside of a wooden salad bowl will keep it from becoming sticky.

- If you cut the root end off the onion last, you'll shed less tears.

- To prevent soggy salads, place an inverted saucer in the bottom of the salad bowl. The excess dressing will drain under the saucer and keep the greens crisp.

- Lettuce and celery will crisp up faster if you add a few raw slices of potato to the cold water you use to soak them.

Sauce Suggestions

- Make sure that flour is well browned before adding it to liquid for gravy. This will prevent lumpy gravy and also assure a rich brown gravy.
- Placing flour in a custard cup in the oven next to the roast will assure nice brown flour for gravy when the meat is done.

Soup and . . .

Soups can be served all alone, and they can be served together with breads, rolls, salads, sandwiches, and crackers. Here are some healthy suggestions that will make your homemade soup meal even more special:

- Sandwiches
- Pita Crisp (recipe at the end of this chapter)
- Green salad
- Corn bread (recipe in children's chapter); great with chili.

Sandwich Ideas

I choose hearty, very nourishing varieties of bread when I serve sandwiches with soup. Listed are some healthy suggestions:

1. Whole wheat pita bread
2. Ezekial bread (or any multi-grain) found in your health food stores.
3. Sprouted wheat
4. Whole Wheat
5. Sprouted rye
6. Pita bread
7. Whole wheat tortillas

Pita Bread Sandwiches

Fill pita bread with any of the following for a tasty accompaniment to any soup meal

1. Turkey salad with sprouts and tomatoes and mayonnaise
2. Creamed cheese with sprouts and cucumbers
3. Refried beans with sliced tomatoes and grated cheese
4. Leftover beans and rice with lettuce, tomato and mayonnaise
5. Egg salad with lettuce, tomato and mayonnaise

Try the following on whole grain bread:

1. Roasted peppers (Mancini brand) and sliced cheese
2. Sliced tomatoes, lettuce, mayonnaise, onions, green peppers, and zucchini
3. Almond butter and spreadable fruit or jelly
4. Almond butter with sliced bananas

CORNEY CORN BREAD

1 cup corn meal (fresh)
2 tablespoons corn oil
¼ cup whole wheat flour
¼ cup pastry wheat flour
¼ teaspoon baking soda
2 yard eggs

¼ teaspoon Sea salt
¼ cup fructose
1 cup milk (low fat)
½ cup corn (cut, fresh)
1 small onion, chopped

Combine first 4 ingredients together. In blender, mix remaining ingredients except corn and onion. Stir in corn and onion. Oil and flour glass pie plate. Bake at 350° for 20 minutes or until slightly brown.

For a sweet corn bread, leave out corn and onion and add one more tablespoon of fructose. For mexican corn bread add 1 finely chopped cubanelle pepper.

HOMEMADE CROUTONS

4 to 6 slices whole wheat bread
4 tablespoons butter
Dash of salt

1 tablespoon your favorite seasoning
1 teaspoon garlic powder

Cut bread into cubes. Lay flat on cookie sheet. Melt butter and stir in garlic and seasoning. Spread butter mixture over bread with basting brush. Bake at 350° for 20 to 30 minutes or until crisp. Leftovers can be stored in airtight container in refrigerator.

PITA CRISPS

Use the same mixture used for croutons. Cut pita bread in half so you have 2 circular pieces. Cut these into quarters like a pie. Place on cookie sheet. Spread on butter mixture with a basting brush. Broil in oven for about 1 minute. Keep your eye on the bread and take out of the oven as soon as it starts to brown. Be careful because it will burn quickly. Makes 8 pita crisps.

NOTES

Delicious
Drinks

Refreshers
Protein Drinks
Shakes and Smoothies

7

Delicious Drinks

Think about your family's nutritional habits. Do you drink coffee, iced tea, and soft drinks all day long? If so, you may be washing away your efforts at good nutrition with every swallow.

Years ago I drank iced tea constantly. I have finally disciplined myself to drink water throughout the day instead. It's possible to have healthy eating habits and continue drinking beverages in a way that undermines our good efforts. A commitment to healthy eating must include a commitment to healthy drinking as well. How we choose to supply liquids to our bodies can be our greatest source of good or poor health.

In this chapter on Delicious Drinks, I have attempted to provide some wonderfully tasty drink recipes as alternatives to the unhealthy liquids that most of us are accustomed to taking into our bodies. I have also attempted to prove some practical advice about our common liquids, such as water and milk. Here's drinking to good health!

Water

Water is the most important liquid we put into our bodies. Since our bodies are made up of approximately seventy-percent water, it's essential that we get enough. As a family, we take water with us wherever we go, and we always have a glass gallon jug of distilled water in our car.

Over the years we finally purchased a water distiller. It was an investment in our family's health and it's the best water I've ever tasted. Unpleasant tasting tap water keeps many individuals from drinking all of the water they should. Some tap water even smells bad. If you have been avoiding drinking water that your body needs because your tap water is unpleasant tasting, why not consider investing in a purifier, or begin purchasing bottled water just for drinking. For more information on water call 1-800-592-HEAL and order the *Maximum Energy* book.

Lemon Water

Lemon water is great for the body, and is very refreshing. I usually drink a glass a day. Squeeze 1 lemon into 8 to 9 ounces of water. If your drink is too tart, just add a little more water. We always order lemon wedges with our water at restaurants because the lemon juice helps to kill any organisms that may be in the water.

Raw Certified Goat's Milk

Does your family drink a lot of milk? Cow's milk is intended for baby cows that need to gain hundreds, even thousands of pounds to reach maturity. It's no wonder milk is so full of heavy fat. The closest milk to mother's milk is raw certified goat's milk. Goat's milk is known as "orphan's milk," meaning that any mammal can be healthily raised on this milk.

Goat's Milk vs. Cow's Milk

Sixty percent of the people in the world drink goat's milk. Noted medical specialist, Carl G. Wilson, M.D., Palo Alto, California, said: "I am convinced that goat milk is the best substitute for human milk in infant feeding, not only because of its close similarity chemically and physically, but because of the readiness with which the infant receives and digests goat's milk. This becomes doubly evident when you compare goat's milk and cow's milk to humans milk.

Cow's milk purchased in the grocery store is pasteurized, which destroys the "friendly bacteria" needed in the colon. It also destroys fluorine, a trace mineral best known for building hardiness of bones and tooth enamel. Raw goat's milk contains ten times as much fluorine as cow's milk.

The fat gobules in goat's milk are five times smaller than those found in cow's milk, which makes it easier to digest. Your baby is not nourished by what he swallows, but only by what his body can digest and assimilate. Cow's milk can also be constipating where raw goat's milk is not, since it contains an abundance of lactic acid. Arthur D. Holmes (Research Professor of Chemistry of Massachusetts) and his co-workers found goat's milk contains desirable amounts of nicotinic and pantothenic acids, riboflavins, and thiamine. (More information on goat's milk in chapter four.) For more information on how to prepare goat milk formula call our office at 1-800-592-HEAL and order "Train Up Your Children in the Way They Should Eat".

Juices

Like anything else, fresh juice is the best. If you can invest in a juicer, you can make your own juice. The best bottled juices can be found in the health food section of your grocery store or your local health food store. These juices are much stronger in flavor and contain pulp, so you may need to dilute them 3 parts water to 1 part juice, which makes them less expensive than the more popular varieties.

Our family loves fresh carrot juice, which is also very nutritious. If you have a juicer, gradually add other vegetables to the carrot juice to find a combination you like. Pure pineapple juice improves the flavor and makes a good base for fresh vegetable juices.

Herbal Teas

Herbal teas are good replacement for former coffee and iced tea drinkers. Tea should never take the place of water in your diet. When purchasing herbal tea, stay away from the oriental teas and the green and black teas, because they contain tannic acid. Also read labels, some herbal teas have been decaffeinated, and it's also best to stay away from these. If you drink decaffeinated tea make sure it's decaffeinated by water process not chemistry.

Coffee

It's always much easier to omit something from your diet that you have been used to eating or drinking most of your life when you have a replacement. I encourage you to limit, or stop drinking caffeinated beverages completely. Several satisfying coffee replacements can be found on the market today. We enjoy Roma by Natural Touch, which is a caffeine-free roasted grain beverage.

If you are a coffee drinker, please read my husband's book, Maximum Energy. He covers caffeine in detail.

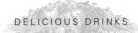

Protein Drinks

Protein drinks are especially beneficial to those who get limited amounts of animal protein in their diets, like vegetarians. Drink a good protein everyday, especially if you are pregnant or exercise regularly.

It's essential to use a high-quality protein powder. The cheapest ones are not always the best. We use a "egg base" protein. A teaspoon of blackstrap molasses can also be added to any of the following drink recipes as an excellent source of iron, which is also easily assimilated by the body.

HIGH NUTRIENT PROTEIN SHAKE

12 ounces water
2 cups frozen, very ripe bananas, peeled and chopped [1 inch pieces] before freezing
2 teaspoons vitamin C powder
2 tablespoons granular lecithin

2 scoops protein powder
1 teaspoon vanilla
1 scoop powered vitamin
1 tablespoon flax seed oil
Frozen fruit (optional)

Combine ingredients in blender. Blend until smooth. To make thicker shake, add more frozen fruit.

BANANA PINEAPPLE COLADA

8 ounces unsweetened pineapple juice
½ cup papaya juice
1 frozen banana

2 ice cubes
1 tablespoon protein powder

Blend until smooth. Serve with a straw.

ORANGE PINEAPPLE DELIGHT

8 ounces unsweetened orange juice

2 slices fresh pineapple

3 ice cubes

1 tablespoon protein powder

2 teaspoon brown rice syrup

Blend until smooth. Serve with a straw.

CRAN-STRAWBERRY SLUSH

8 ounce pure cranberry juice
  (Lakewood is an excellent brand)

1 tablespoon protein powder

4 to 5 frozen strawberries

½ cup unfiltered apple juice

3 ice cubes

Blend until smooth. Serve with a straw.

APPLE CINNAMON DELIGHT

8 ounces unfiltered apple juice

1 tablespoon protein powder

Dash of cinnamon

2 to 3 frozen strawberries

3 ice cubes

Blend until smooth. Serve with a straw.

STRAWBERRY PINEAPPLE SMOOTHIE

8 ounces unsweetened pineapple juice

1 tablespoon protein powder

2 slices fresh pineapple

2 to 3 frozen strawberries*

Blend until smooth. Serve with a straw.

*Frozen fruit with no sugar added can be purchased at most grocery stores.

SUMMER COOLER

1 cup water
4 cups unsweetened pineapple juice
½ cup unsweetened orange juice

Juice of 2 lemons
3 lemon slices

Mix all ingredients together in pitcher. Add lemon slices and serve over ice.

AUTUMN COOLER

4 cups water
2 cups unfiltered apple juice

1½ cups unsweetened cranberry juice
(Lakewood is an excellent brand)

Mix all ingredients together and serve over ice.

STRAWBERRY MILKSHAKE

2 cups low fat milk or goat's milk
½ tablespoon protein powder (optional)
2 frozen bananas

1 tablespoon vanilla
2 tablespoons maple syrup
Frozen strawberries

Combine milk, protein, vanilla, blackstrap, and sweetener in blender. Add fruit until desired thickness. Serve with a straw.

PEACH MILKSHAKE

Make the same recipe as the Strawberry Shake but replace the frozen peaches for the strawberries.

CAROB BANANA SHAKE

2 tablespoons carob powder

3 frozen bananas

2 tablespoons maple syrup

1 teaspoon vanilla

2 cups milk

1 cup crushed ice

Combine bananas and milk in blender; blend until smooth. Add carob powder, then syrup and vanilla; blend until smooth. Add ice for desired thickness. **Serves 4**.

FROSTY FIZZ

¼ cup favorite fruit juice sparkler
  or spritzer

2 tablespoons vanilla ice cream
  (Haagan-Dazs or Bryer's)

Pour juice in large glass. Add ice cream.

WEIGHT GAIN MILK SHAKE

2 cups milk or goat's milk

1 tablespoon vanilla

2 tablespoons protein powder

1 tablespoon blackstrap molasses

1 tablespoon fructose

2 tablespoons natural almond butter
  (or peanut butter)

2 to 3 frozen bananas

1 tablespoon carob powder (optional)

In blender, mix milk, vanilla, protein, blackstrap, and sweetener. Add nut butter gradually until smooth. Add banana, then carob. Blend until smooth. **Makes 2 large shakes**.

This is very high in calories.

BLUE STRAWBERRY SHAKE

1 cup concord grape juice

1 cup unprocessed apple juice

1 cup frozen blueberries (no sugar added)

1 cup frozen strawberries

2 cups crushed ice

Combine fruit and juices in blender. Blend until smooth. Add ice slowly until desired thickness. **Serves 6**.

HOT CREAMY CAROB

2½ cups goat's milk (or hormone-
free milk)

2 tablespoons Brown rice syrup (add
according to taste)

2 tablespoon carob powder

1 teaspoon vanilla

Mix all ingredients in saucepan. Bring to a boil. Remove from heat and add vanilla. **Serves 2**.

EGGNOG

See chapter eleven.

HOT CHRISTMAS PUNCH CIDER

See chapter eleven.

NOTES

Delightful Desserts

Creative Yummy Cookies
Frosty Favorites
Fabulous Fudge

8

Delightful Desserts

Eating healthily doesn't mean you cannot enjoy delightfully tempting desserts. In this chapter you will find fabulous dessert recipes with all of the wonderful flavors you are used to enjoying — but without the guilt!

Note: When I am short on time I use Simple Organic mixes as a base.

CAROB MACAROONS

⅓ cup whole wheat pastry flour   ¼ cup almonds, chopped
    1 cup coconut (shredded, unsweetened)   8 ounces carob soymilk
    1 tablespoon carob powder   1 tablespoon coffee substitute
    2 tablespoons fructose   1 teaspoon vanilla

In small bowl combine whole wheat pastry flour, almonds, and coconut; mix well. In saucepan mix milk, carob and fructose. Bring to a boil, while stirring for 5 minutes. Remove from burner. Add coffee substitute and vanilla. Mix well. Add flour mixture to carob mixture. Mix well. Drop by large tablespoons on greased cookie sheet. Bake for 10 minutes at 350°.

CAROB CHIP COOKIES

    1 egg   ½ cup fructose
    1 ¼ cups whole wheat pastry flour   6 tablespoons butter, softened
    1 teaspoon baking powder   1 teaspoon vanilla
    ½ cup carob chips

In blender combine egg and butter; blend until smooth. Add sweeteners and vanilla. In large bowl mix together remaining ingredients. Combine blender mixture with dry ingredients. Mix well. Fold in carob chips. Drop on cookie sheets by teaspoons. Bake at 350° for 10 to 12 minutes. **Makes 3 dozen**.

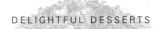

WHOLE WHEAT OATMEAL COOKIES

2 cups whole wheat pastry flour	½ teaspoon cinnamon
¾ teaspoon baking powder	½ cup fructose
1 teaspoon vanilla	½ teaspoon baking soda
1¼ cups rolled oats	6 tablespoons butter
½ cup pecans, chopped	2 eggs

In large bowl combine all dry ingredients. In blender, mix together butter and sweeteners. Add eggs, cinnamon, and vanilla. Stir in with dry ingredients.

Mix well. Stir in pecans. On cookie sheet, drop one teaspoon of batter for each cookie. Bake at 350° for 10 to 12 minutes. **Makes 4 dozen**.

GRANOLA COOKIES

Dedicated to Beth Hunt, a missionary in Costa Rica.

½ cup water	1 teaspoon Baking soda
2 eggs	1 cup butter
2½ cups whole wheat pastry flour	½ cup fructose
1½ cups rolled oats	2 teaspoons vanilla
1 cup chopped pecans	1 teaspoon cinnamon
1 cup unsweetened shredded coconut	1 teaspoon baking powder

In large bowl, combine flour and all dry ingredients. Mix well. In blender, combine eggs, butter, water, and vanilla. Blend well. Gradually stir in dry ingredients, pecans, coconut. On greased cookie sheet, drop 1 teaspoon of batter for each cookie. Bake 10 to 12 minutes at 350°. **Yield: 5 dozen**.

GRANOLA BARS

2 eggs	1 teaspoon baking soda
2 cup granola cereal	½ cup rolled oats
¾ cup butter	2 teaspoons vanilla
1 tablespoon blackstrap molasses	1 teaspoon cinnamon
2 cups whole wheat pastry flour	¾ cup fructose

Preheat oven to 300°. In blender mix together eggs, butter, sweeteners, and vanilla. In large bowl mix together remaining ingredients. Stir in liquid ingredients from blender. Press in a 12-by-18-by-1-inch cookie pan or a pan of equal size. Bake at 300° for 15 minutes, checking the bars to make sure they do not burn on the bottom. Let cool and cut into 2-by-3 inch bars. **Serves 12**.

REFRIGERATOR CRUNCHIES

1 cup dried apricots, chopped	¼ cup raisins
½ cup pecans, chopped	2 tablespoons orange juice
1½ cups water	

Bring water to a boil. Pour over apricots and raisins. Let drain for at least 30 minutes. Stir in pecans and orange juice. Shape into balls and refrigerate.

GRANANA BITES

4 mashed bananas	¾ cup favorite crunchy cereal or
½ cup rolled oats	granola
¾ cup chopped nuts	1 teaspoon vanilla

Add all ingredients to bananas; mix well. Drop onto ungreased cookie sheet about the size of a teaspoon. Bake at 350° for 30 minutes. **Makes about 30 cookies**.

BANANA FINGERS

4 bananas (firm but ripe)   1 cup natural vanilla yogurt
1 cup unsweetened coconut (shredded)   1 cup pecans, chopped

Cut each banana into thirds. Dip each banana in yogurt, then roll in coconut, then roll in pecans. Store in refrigerator. This is also a good party snack or for large groups. **Serves 10 to 12**.

MOCK GERMAN CHOCOLATE BIRTHDAY CAKE

2 cups unbleached flour   ½ cup fructose
1 cup carob powder   1 cup brown rice syrup
2 teaspoons baking powder   1 cup butter, softened
4 eggs   2 teaspoons vanilla

In large bowl, combine flour, carob, and baking powders. In blender, combine butter and sweeteners. Blend until smooth. Slightly beat eggs, then add to blender with remaining ingredients. Mix with dry ingredients. Pour into 2 greased and floured pans. Bake at 350° for 20 to 25 minutes. **Serves 12 to 14**.

MOCK GERMAN CHOCOLATE ICING

1 cup non-instant powdered dry milk   ¼ cup water
4 tablespoons softened butter   2 teaspoons vanilla
½ cup pecans, finely chopped   ½ cup brown rice syrup
½ cup unsweetened shredded coconut   2 tablespoons carob powder

With electric mixer, blend butter and syrup. Add carob powder and vanilla. Slowly add milk powder while mixing with water. When icing is creamy, add coconut and pecans. Ice when cake has cooled.

NUT BUTTER BALLS

1 cup nut butter (peanut, almond
   or cashew)
1 teaspoon vanilla
1½ cups crispy rice cereal
1 cup nuts, chopped

½ cup maple syrup
1 teaspoon cinnamon
1 cup oat bran
½ cup coconut (optional)

Mix together nut butter, syrup, vanilla, and cinnamon in large bowl. Stir in cereal and oat bran. (I find it easier to mix it with my hands since it's so thick.) When completely mixed form into about 1-inch balls and place on waxed paper. Take each individual ball and roll in nuts and/or coconut. Chill in refrigerator. Place 5 or 6 in individual bags. Store in freezer. Thaw in refrigerator and eat as snacks.

CREAMY CARROT CAKE

4 eggs
1 cup softened butter
1 cup fructose
2½ cups whole wheat pastry flour
1 teaspoon cinnamon

1 teaspoon orange peel, grated
2 teaspoons vanilla
1 teaspoon baking soda
2½ cups grated carrots
1 teaspoon baking powder

In blender, mix eggs and butter. Add vanilla and blend well. Stir in carrots. In large bowl combine remaining ingredients. Mix well. Slowly stir in ingredients from blender. Butter and flour a 9-by-13-inch baking dish. Bake at 350° for 45 to 50 minutes.

PECAN 'N SPICE ICING

¼ cup softened butter

¼ cup fructose

1 teaspoon vanilla

½ cup unsweetened shredded coconut

1 cup pecans, chopped

⅛ teaspoon ground cloves

2 tablespoons water

1 cup non-instant dry milk

With electric mixer, combine butter, fructose, cinnamon, cloves, and vanilla; mix until creamy. Slowly add dry milk. Add water as needed to thick icing. When icing is smooth, add coconut and pecans. Ice cooled cake. **Serves 12**.

GRANOLA BIRTHDAY CAKE

4 cups whole wheat pastry flour

3 cups granola cereal

1 tablespoon Baking powder

2 ripe bananas

1 cup butter

1 tablespoon vanilla

1 tablespoon cinnamon

½ tablespoon ground allspice

2 cups unfiltered apple juice

½ cup fructose

Preheat oven to 350°. Mix together all dry ingredients. In blender, combine butter and remaining ingredients; add to dry ingredients. Blend until smooth. Pour into 3 buttered cake pans. Bake for 25 minutes or until inserted toothpick comes out clean. Cool for 15 minutes, then remove from pans. Allow cakes to cool, then spread icing between layers and on top.

Icing:

½ cup carob powder

½ cup fructose

½ cup butter

½ cup unsweetened shredded coconut

Melt butter and fructose in a double boiler. Slowly add carob until thick enough to spread. Add coconut. Spread icing. This recipe can be used as large sheet cake. Pour batter in extra large baking dish. Serve with or without icing.

YUM CONES

24 flat ice cream cup cones (I use a
    brand from the natural food store)
⅓ cup butter
⅛ cup honey
1 teaspoon vanilla
2 teaspoons baking powder

Vanilla yogurt (optional)
½ cup crunchy peanut butter
2 eggs
2 cups whole wheat flour
¾ cup low-fat milk

Beat together butter, peanut butter, and honey. Beat in eggs and vanilla. Add remaining ingredients and beat until well mixed. Spoon into cones ¾ full. Bake at 350° for 25 minutes. Spread yogurt over top after cooled.

MELON SICKLES

4 cups watermelon, cut up
Plastic ice cube trays

Popsicle sticks

Remove seeds from melon. In blender mix melon until smooth. Pour into ice cube trays. Place in freezer. When almost frozen place sticks in cubes. Freeze until solid.

FROZEN GRAPES

Wash fresh Thompson seedless grapes and place in airtight container in freezer. Makes a great cold summer snack. Good replacement for ice cream.

BANANA POPS

4 bananas
8 popsicle sticks

½ cup brown rice syrup
1 cup natural granola

Cut each banana into two pieces. Spread rice syrup on each banana and roll in granola. Freeze and store in airtight container. **Serves 8**.

JUICE POPS

2 cups unprocessed apple juice   1 cup unsweetened cranberry juice
1. cup unsweetened black cherry juice

Mix juices in blender. Pour into plastic ice cube trays. Freeze until almost frozen. Insert Popsicle sticks and allow to completely freeze. I like to use Tupperware Popsicle holders for added convenience.

BLUEBERRY DELIGHT

4 cups fresh blueberries   1 cup water
½ cup non-instant dry milk   3 tablespoons sorghum

In blender combine milk and water; mix well. Add sorghum. In bowl, mix together blueberries and milk mixture. Spoon into 4 individual dessert bowls or glasses. Place in freezer for 1 hour. Top with natural whipped topping. **Serves 4**.

NATURAL WHIPPED TOPPING

½ cup milk powder   2 tablespoons maple syrup
½ cup ice water

Combine milk powder and water in chilled bowl. Beat with electric mixer for about 5 minutes, until peaks form. Add maple syrup and beat for 5 more minutes. Use within 2 hours.

APPLESAUCE

6 large firm apples, cored   ½ cup unprocessed apple juice
1 tablespoon cinnamon

Chop up apples in cubes. In blender combine apples and juice. Blend until smooth. Add cinnamon. **Serves 4**.

BROWN APPLE BROER

6 cup sliced apples   ½ cup apple juice
2 teaspoons cinnamon

Place apples in baking dish. Mix together juice and cinnamon; pour over apples.

Topping:

½ cup whole wheat flour   1 tablespoon blackstrap molasses
¼ cup fructose   2 teaspoons cinnamon
1 cup rolled oats   3 tablespoons butter
½ cup granola cereal   ½ cup pecans, chopped
¼ cup maple syrup   2 tablespoons apple juice

Mix together all ingredients and crumble over apples. Bake at 350° for 40 minutes. **Serves 6**.

BAKED APPLES

4 apples, washed and cored   1 teaspoon cinnamon
¼ cup water   1 teaspoon maple syrup
1 teaspoon butter

Place apples in baking dish. Pour water in bottom of dish. Mix together butter, maple syrup, and cinnamon; pour into center of apples. Bake at 350° for 1 hour. Top with chopped walnuts. **Serves 4**.

MAKE AHEAD TOPPING

This is good to make a big batch and store in Ziploc bag in freezer. Use any in season baked fruit. This topping will make a delicious combo with your fruit.

1 cup whole wheat flour	½ cup unsweetened shredded coconut
2 tablespoons melted butter	1 teaspoon vanilla
1 cup pecans, chopped	

Combine all ingredients in large bowl and mix thoroughly. Crumble over sliced apples or peaches. Bake at 350° for 20 minutes or until top is golden brown.

Have you ever tried yogurt dessert? Make Ahead Topping is also great with yogurt for dessert anytime.

CRUNCHY YOGURT:

1 cup "Make Ahead Topping", baked and cooled	Yogurt

Use any flavor yogurt and use preceding recipe as a crunchy topping

BANANA PUDDING

2 boxes Frookie brand vanilla wafers	6 to 8 sliced bananas
3 large containers Kozy Shack pre-made pudding (found in refrigerator section)	6 egg whites
	4 to 6 tablespoons fructose

Prepare pudding following directions on cartons. (I use ½ cup less milk for 2 cartons so pudding will be firmer.) In medium oblong (13-by-9-inch) casserole dish place vanilla wafers enough to cover bottom. Pour half of pudding over wafers. Slice bananas over top of pudding. Repeat this layering one more time. Refer to page 55 for the meringue recipe.

STRAWBERRY JELLO

2 cups unprocessed apple juice   1 cup fresh strawberries
3 tablespoons gelatin

In saucepan mix together gelatin and ½ cup apple juice. Simmer over medium heat for 5 minutes, continually stirring. Stir in remaining juice. In blender lightly blend strawberries together. Stir in strawberries with gelatin mixture. Pour into dish and refrigerate until firm. **Serves 4**.

FUN FRUIT FOLLIES

3 (¼ ounce) package unflavored gelatin   1 can orange juice (frozen concentrate)
¾ cup boiling water

Dissolve gelatin in boiling water. Add concentrate and mix well. Pour into lightly sprayed (cooking spray) 9-by-13-inch dish. Refrigerate for several hours. Use your children's' favorite shape cookie cutters for fun fruit follies

ALMOND CAROB FUDGE

3 tablespoons raw butter   3 tablespoons carob powder
½ cup skim milk   1 cup fructose

Combine preceding ingredients in saucepan. Bring to a boil. Boil for 1 minute, stirring constantly. Remove from heat.

Have standing by:

1½ cups almond butter or nut butter   1 cup unsweetened shredded
3 cups natural rolled oats   coconuts (optional)
1 teaspoon vanilla

Stir in remaining ingredients with carob mixture in order that they are listed. Mix well and place in large glass baking dish. Press in bottom of dish. Refrigerate for 1 hour. Cut into square. **Serves 12**.

^{A}Child's _Diet_

Breast Feeding and Alternatives
Baby Food Recipes
A.D.D Diet
"Let's Do Lunch" Kids
Fun Foods
Sandwich Ideas

9

A Child's Diet

Do you accept the misery of occasional colds, runny noses, bronchial infections, and coughs as a normal, expected part of childhood? You don't have to. It's possible to have children who feel really good, whose precious little faces radiate a glow of health.

Our entire family enjoys genuinely good health. But it's no accident. Giving our children good health takes time, discipline, and a little extra commitment. But having children who feel great is a blessing — and well worth the extra effort.

Make your child's nutritional health a top priority. With all the fast and convenient foods we have available to us, it is so much easier to go with the majority of Americans who cook and grocery shop for convenience. It saves time, but you only have to sit with a sick child once to decide that convenience is not worth the price of our children's good health.

No treasure is so precious as genuinely good health, and you can give this wonderful gift to your children. However, starting as early as possible is a vital key. If you bless your children with good nutrition in the cradle, vitality and health can follow them to the grave. So let's start at the very beginning.

Infant Nutrition

I have read and been told many times that it is best to nurse your baby for two years. This "valuable" advice is usually given by a male who has no idea what it is like to even nurse one year. I nursed my son for nine months and I admit that it was a challenge. I had really wanted to nurse for a full year, but since I had to run our office, it got to be too much stress. If you lead a stress-free life with no demands on you, you can probably nurse 1½ to 2 years.

Since a baby's digestive system is so sensitive, it is best to wait as long as possible before introducing any type of solid food. If the infant is not staying satisfied with mother's milk and it's too early to introduce cereal, etc., try out homemade goat's milk formula.

For more detailed information, I recommend my book, *Train Up Your Children in the Way They Should Eat*. This book is an absolute must if you have children. It will take you through in detail proper infant formula from birth to weaning.

Now, before leaving this subject of goat's milk, I want to offer one more item from Dr. Jensen about this wonderful food for your baby.

Some years ago, the Journal of the American Medical Association published an article titled "Dietetics and Hygiene", which reported: "The goat is the healthiest domestic animal known. Goat milk is superior in every respect to cow's milk. Goat milk is the ideal food for babies, convalescents, and invalids, especially those with weakened digestive powers. Goat milk is the purest, most healthful, and most complete food known."

Cow's milk is much harder to digest than goat's milk, plus the cows are injected with hormones and antibiotics and then the milk is homogenized and pasteurized, killing all the natural digestive enzymes that help in digestion and absorption. Cow's milk is made for baby cows which are much bigger than a precious baby. No wonder so many children are having allergies to milk.

Goat's milk is the closest milk to mother's milk. It is called the "orphan food". The best way to find fresh goat's milk in your area is to find people who raise goats. Ask around at your farm and garden centers or even your health food stores may know. I will not buy goat's milk at the grocery store or health food stores since I have noticed the taste is too strong. If you buy raw goat's milk straight from the goat's owners, it's much fresher. Goat's milk can be frozen up to 6 months also, so if you have a long drive to where you purchase your milk (like we do), you may want to stock up. When given to a baby "raw", the enzyme phospertase is still available in the milk, which helps the body absorb the calcium in the milk. Another live enzyme in "raw" goat's milk is fluorine, which is nature's natural source of fluoride.

If this is the first thing introduced to the infant besides mother's milk, you will need to keep an eye on the skin for any redness or diaper rash. You may need to cut back on the amount of goat's milk you are giving to your baby or you may need to introduce the milk at another time.

To Nurse or Not to Nurse: That is the Question

In the 1940's and the 1950's the "bottle revolution" in feeding babies broke out. Doctors and so-called "modern" mothers had argued that breast feeding was inconvenient, nutritionally unreliable, and too time consuming. Today, more and more benefits are becoming more widely recognized.

Breast Feeding Benefits the Mother

- The suckling of the newborn stimulates the release of the hormone that stimulates the shrinking of the mother's uterus back to normal.
- Nursing usually develops a close emotional bond between the mother and the child.

Breast Feeding Benefits the Baby

- Mother's milk provides the baby with the right kind of digestible proteins.
- The baby has fewer colds and less colic when breast fed.

The Importance of Colostrum

Colostrum is the substance formed in the mother's mammary glands before the baby is born. It is the milk given the first three days of nursing that passes along the mother's immunity toward certain disease to her newborn baby. It is the most important nutrient a newborn will ever get.

Colostrum contains substances that destroy viruses. It starts proper bowel movements that furnish the important acidophilus bacteria to the baby's bowels.

Researchers have estimated that colostrum triggers at least fifty processes and functions in the newborn that provide lasting benefits.

Being a non-milk, colostrum is much higher in protein and has ten to seventeen times the iron content of milk, three times as much Vitamin D, and ten times more Vitamin A. Immunoglobulins from which antibodies are formed make up the majority of protein in colostrum.

What if I Cannot Breast Feed My Baby?

Hopefully, by now you are starting to understand the importance of nursing your baby. However, not every mother is able to nurse for one reason or another. Sometimes the mother may have some type of problem with her nipples or some type of medical problem. If you are adopting your baby and are not taking special herb to cause milk, you may also need some alternatives.

Good News for Non-Nursing Mothers!

My first choice for a mother with a newborn is to breast feed her baby. If she can't, I have good news. Research has found that colostrum from cows or goats is much more potent than human colostrum. Cow colostrum is processed, dried into a powder, and is now being made available to the public. Virtually all other mammals, including man, accept bovine colostrum. The disease resistant factors in the colostrum are simply transferred to the person (or animal) that uses it. When using cow's colostrum, make sure the source is from selected, pre-tested, disease free, registered, grade A dairy cows that have given birth to at least three calves.

CEREALS

First: Grind up enough grains for about a two week supply of cereal.

4 cup brown rice	½ cup millet
1½ cups whole wheat	½ cup barley
1 cup rye wheat	½ cup buckwheat

Second: Take four 1 quart jars with secure lids for cereal.

No. 1 – Cream of Wheat

1 cup brown rice	1 cup whole wheat

No. 2 – Cream of Buckwheat

1 cup brown rice	½ cup buckwheat
½ cup rye	

No. 3 – Cream of Millet

1 cup brown rice	½ cup whole wheat
½ cup millet	

No. 4 – Cream of Barley

1 cup brown rice	½ cup rye
½ cup barley	

Mix each combination in the jar, secure lid, and store in freezer.

Helpful Hints to Cooking Hot Cereals

1. Always add ground grains to water while water is cold. If you add to boiling water, the cereal will be very lumpy.

2. Most grains cook up good by using a 1–3 ratio (example: 2½ cups water to ½ cup of grains). If grains are too thick, just add more water.

3. Always bring cereal to a boil. It may have a thinner texture until it cools. The longer it cooks, the thicker it gets.

4. Remember, babies are not born with a "sweet tooth". Don't think you have to sweeten your baby's cereals to "your taste". At this age they start developing their taste habits. Why make them want sugar when they don't know the difference?

5. When adding any sweetener, start with the least sweetest as your first choice.
   Least sweetest: Barley malt syrup, brown rice syrup, sorghum molasses, maple syrup, Fructose.
   Sweetest: Honey.

Ingredients to Add to Cereal

Vanilla extract	Unsweetened shredded coconut
Oat bran	Blackstrap molasses (great
Banana extract	source of iron)
Dried fruit	Powder vitamin supplement
Mashed banana (after	Only a little bit to start with
baby's teeth come in)	(⅛ to ¼ teaspoon.; can be added
Maple extract	if baby is not nursing)

Quick Ways to Cool Cereal

I realize making hot cereals in the morning does take time. I have found the time is in waiting for the cereal to cool so your children can eat it. Try this:

- If cereal is extra thick, add an ice cube and stir
- Serve up cereal in individual bowls and place in freezer. (Remember it's in there!)

Starting on Pureed Foods

When you start your baby on pureed foods (about 7 to 10 months), it is best to keep him on them for as long as possible. Pureed food is very easy to digest. The easier the food is for the baby to digest means less problems with digestion and absorption. Until a baby has most of his molars, the food can't be chewed well enough to digest properly, causing baby not to get the total amount of energy from the food.

We are so blessed today to have available to us several companies that manufacture organic baby food. When it comes to saving money in your family budget, you should avoid trying to cut corners on baby food. Your baby is worth the best. If you want to cut back on other items, do so, but buy the very best for your baby.

The availability of organic baby food has made it so convenient for mothers who want the purest and most nutritious food possible for their babies. The preparation time for the baby's food alone is an incredible bonus.

I personally prefer "Earth's Best" baby food. This company was the first in the baby food industry to introduce organic baby food. Now, other companies have followed in the footsteps of Earth's Best, realizing the demand for pesticide and chemical free baby food. Other companies include Organic Baby, and now even Gerber Baby Food Company has awakened to the need of organic baby food with their line of Healthy Harvest.

If you find you have the time, or you have fruit and vegetables from your family meals, I suggest you make your own baby food also. A baby food grinder may be purchased for $6 to $8. Using a grinder enables you to instantly puree your baby's food at the table.

When feeding your baby more solid foods, check the diaper and if the food is going through the baby whole or practically whole, this is a good indication the baby does not have enough teeth to properly chew the food for proper digestion.

Sweet Potatoes

Wash and peel potatoes. Slice into ½ inch pieces. Place in pan and cover with distilled water. Add ¼ teaspoon of blackstrap molasses. Bring water to a boil and simmer until potatoes are tender. Place potatoes in blender and reserve water. Add just enough water so potatoes will puree. Baby food will thicken when it cools. Spoon into individual baby food jars.

Split Peas and Rice

½ cup brown rice   1½ cups split peas
4½ cups water

Bring peas and rice to a boil. Simmer for 1 hour. Pour into blender and add just enough water to puree but not so much that it becomes runny. Puree and pour into jars and refrigerate.

Beets

4 cups beets, washed, peeled, and   Water
    sliced into ½ inch pieces

Place beets in saucepan with water. Bring to a boil and simmer until tender (insert fork). Reserve water. To add more nutrients, cook beet tops in with the beets. Place in blender with just enough water to puree. Pour into jars and refrigerate.

Green Beans and Rice

½ cup brown rice, cooked   Water
3 cups greens, cooked

Save any greens you have cooked for dinner. Reserve the water. Puree in blender with just enough water to mix well. Pour in jars and refrigerate.

In place of the greens, you can use squash, green beans, peas, black-eyes peas, broccoli, or any cooked beans.

A Child's Diet

It has always been a pleasant challenge to work with mothers on the subject of feeding their children. We must understand several things about children and their relationship to food before any of the following information can be used effectively.

"Training up a child" in all aspects of his life includes training them to eat in the healthiest way possible. Along with all the other learning experiences in a child's life, food and diet should be treated with love and discipline. Children need to know they are loved, and discipline is a way of showing love.

Until a child reaches a certain age, he is not used to making very many decisions on his own, but he can make choices. For instance, a six-year- old cannot be sent to a clothing store and be expected to buy his new clothes for school. He is not at the age that he can make the proper decision, but mom and dad can decided on the clothes, and then the child may be given a choice of which outfit he would like to wear to school. The parents have made the decision and the child can be given a choice. A child's diet should be treated in the same way.

The mother (if she is the one preparing the family meals), has the responsibility to make the most nutritious decisions in meal planning. Whenever possible, she should try to give her children a choice. When taking this approach, the child is less likely to rebel, and you can be assured you are being fair.

The Lord has made us people of habit and a child develops habits immediately in life. This is why Proverbs says, "Train up a child in the way he should go; and when he is old he will not depart from it." From day one, if your children are raised on the most nutritious foods you can feed them, they will develop a habit and taste for these foods. This is why breast milk is so important in the life of a newborn baby. Nursing a child is not only best for the child's health, but it is also important physically and emotionally for both mother and child.

Today, America is raising the weakest generation of children we have ever seen. More and more "mothers-to-be" are starting to realize that a healthy child cannot be made with soda pop and snack cakes. If we take a look at the average American's diet, we have no problem understanding why our children are being born with allergies, diabetes, and cancer. If this information comes as a shock to you, it's because it is not a positive subject. Once you have the knowledge, you have no excuse.

I have always heard that a woman should start preparing her body for pregnancy at least one year before conception. I personally believe (if possible) a woman should start preparing for pregnancy at least two years before conception. Back in the early 1900's I really don't think it mattered as much, but today we really need to "clean up" our diets. It took me almost two years of eating all the "right foods" and drinking water, to get my sugar levels to consistent normal levels. Does this help you realize why juvenile diabetes is sky rocketing? Your baby is a sum total of the food and drink you feed your cells during pregnancy. Healthy cells cannot be made from hamburgers, French fries, colas, etc. Cells need vitamins, minerals, and protein for proper growth.

When a woman eats during pregnancy, she is eating to sustain one life and develop another. The diet for mother-to-be should consist of fresh grains, nuts, seeds, vegetables, and fruit along with distilled water. She should supplement her diet with a high quality calcium product along with a non-petroleum base multiple vitamin with one hundred percent of biotin and iron. Also a high quality protein drink should be included.

God will honor your months of persistence and discipline. I pray that this cookbook can be a helpful tool in developing your "picture of health," beautiful, bouncing baby.

Those of you that have the privilege of introducing new and more nutritious foods to your older youngsters, hang on, there is hope! In the process of changing children's diets, you must remember that they are probably not as excited about this new way of eating as you are, yet they do respond much more quickly to diet change than adults. Just remember, "you can't whip a U-turn with the Queen Mary." If you prefer less rebellion and more cooperation from your children, there are a few points you many want to keep in mind.

- You are setting the example: your children are going to keep a very close watch on what goes in your mouth. Don't expect your children to eat more fruit instead of candy, if you don't. The families I have worked with, who have had little or no rebellion are always those whose parents strictly watch their diets even when the children aren't around.

- Sit your child down and explain (on their level) what a good diet and bad diet can do. Explain to them what happens when children get diabetes. Explain to your children how the people on TV commercials are not concerned about his health. Tell them what excess sugar does to the body.

- Make meal time a positive and exciting time for your children. Make it something they can look forward to on a daily basis. Let your children help in the preparation of a meal (even if it's something small). An example: Try using chop sticks one night when you serve stir-fry. This makes the meal fun and children love fun.

- Try to make your meals as colorful as possible. You should serve "new" recipes no more than once a week; two at the most. Your children (and spouse) will figure out very quickly that "Monday night is Mom's weird recipe night". Make sure you serve your new recipes on different nights of the week instead of the same nights each week.

- Encourage your children to eat as much salad as they will eat. You can put your child's favorite vegetables in the salad and offer them a wide choice of dressings from which they can choose.

- Most children love bread. Too much bread is not good. It adds lots of calories as well as having a tendency to be constipating. Try to replace most of the bread consumption with corn bread, which has a very high mineral content.

- Variety is the key in eating a balanced diet. It is more important to be concerned about the variety of foods your child is eating rather than the quantity.

- Keep in mind, as a child is growing, we must remember his organs are still growing and developing. A child's digestive system along with the digestive juices gets stronger as the child matures. Animal meat can put stress on the digestive system. These types of foods require a tremendous amount of digestive juices to be properly digested.

- Chocolate is also very hard on the digestive system, especially on the kidneys. Carob powder or carob chips are a great replacement, in moderation. (when purchasing carob chips, make sure they are made without hydrogenated oil.)
- Don't teach your child to use the salt shaker. (See vegetable chapter for salt replacements.)
- Try to limit your child's snacking before bedtime. Avoid a habit of eating sweets every evening. This may help prevent bed wetting and hyperactivity.
- Avoid excess intake of cheese in your child's diet. It is very high in fat and may cause constipation.

Foods to avoid in a Child's Diet

- Nuts and nut butters before age six (very hard to digest)
- Meat before the age of ten (hardest food to digest) — Daniel 1:3-16
- Processed cereals
- Chocolate (hard to digest and hard on the kidneys)
- Margarine (the chemical process causes trans-fats which cause a rise in cholesterol and triglycerides)
- White sugar
- White Bread (homemade corn bread is excellent)

Foods to be Eaten in Moderation

- White potatoes (acts as a sugar in the body)
- Fruit late in the afternoon or evening
- Watermelon (may cause frequent urination)
- Bread (can be very constipating plus cause weight gain)
- Cheese (also can be very constipating plus cause weight gain)
- Carob

A.D.D.
(Attention Deficit Disorders)

When my first cookbook was published fourteen years ago, information on Attention Deficit Disorder was not even a subject that needed addressing. Most of the problems that children were experiencing then, when my husband was seeing around forty people a day, were corrected by changing the diet of the children.

Today, America is one of the few countries which even suffers from this disorder. The language of some countries does not even have a term for children who are out of control because the country does not have that problem. Before you spend time and money on this subject, first make sure the problem is not due to a lack of consistent discipline. If you believe that is not the issue, then you should next examine your child's diet.

Before you decide to put your child on a drug like Ritalin, first start eliminating foods that cause "Food Sensitivity Reactions in Hyperactive Children." Some of these foods or additives are listed as follows: Red dye, yellow dye, blue dye, colorings and preservatives, cow's milk, chocolate, white sugar, honey, corn sweeteners, and fruit juices.

If your child has symptoms related to A.D.D., I suggest you order my husband's book, *Maximum Solutions to A.D.D. & A.D.H.D.* 1-800-592-HEAL.

I think the most asked question I receive from mothers is "What do I give my child for lunch?" Well, I'm glad you asked.

Hey Kids, Let's Do Lunch!

When all else fails, there is always the "good old American sandwich", peanut butter and jelly. Remember, I'm talking about good whole grain bread (without bad oil and preservatives) and good peanut butter (no hydrogenated oil — just peanuts and salt). This should be eaten in moderation and should not be eaten if weight gain is a problem.

CREATIVE P.B.J.'S

Peanut butter and raisins on whole wheat
Peanut butter and dried fruit on whole wheat
Peanut butter and applesauce on whole wheat
Peanut butter and granola on whole wheat
Peanut butter and coconut on whole wheat
Peanut butter and carrots on whole wheat
Peanut butter and bananas on whole wheat
Peanut butter and apple slices on whole wheat

COOKIE CUTTER SANDWICHES

1 large metal cookie cutter (one that will use up a whole piece of bread)

2 pieces bread (whole grain)

Remember, kids judge food by the presentation. They are more likely to try something new if it looks fun.

For example: Use a large teddy bear cookie cutter and use raisins for the eyes.

Sandwich Ideas

For school lunches, it's best to make sandwiches the night before and tightly store in refrigerator. When you put sandwiches in a lunchbox with a lunchbox cooler, the sandwich stays much cooler.

Try these:

Cream cheese instead of mayonnaise
Pita bread instead of loaf bread
Whole wheat tortilla shells instead of bread

AUSTIN BROER'S SPECIAL SANDWICH

(invented at age 9)

1 whole wheat tortillas	1 can beans (refried)
½ can bean dip	Dash of garlic powder
Dash of salt	Grated cheese

Mix together beans and bean dip and 2 tablespoons of grated cheese. Add salt and garlic to taste. Spread on tortillas. (Put remaining bean mixture in airtight container and store in refrigerator.) Top with grated cheese. Roll up tortilla, heat in microwave until cheese starts to slightly melt and serve.

PRETZELS

1 package active dry yeast	2½ cup pastry flour (unbleached)
1½ cups water (105⁰ to 115⁰ warm)	1 cup Cheddar cheese, grated
1 cup whole wheat flour	1 beaten egg

Dissolve yeast in water. Stir in flour and cheese. Knead dough about 15 to 20 times. Dough should not be very sticky. Add a dash of flour to firm up dough if sticky. Roll dough into pieces about 12 to 14 inches long and ½ inch thick. Let children make pretzel shape or make their own initials. Bake at 350° until golden brown, 10 to 15 minutes.

CONFETTI POTATO CHIPS

2 baking potatoes   Salt
2 sweet potatoes

Slice potatoes paper thin (about ⅟₁₆ inch thick). Arrange on an oiled cookie sheet. Salt lightly. Bake at 400° for 15 to 20 minutes. Enjoy!

POPULAR POPCORN

Cheese and Garlic:

1 clove garlic, minced   2 tablespoons grated Parmesan
1 teaspoon olive oil   cheese
1 teaspoon dried parsley   1 big bowl popped corn

In small saucepan, sauté oil and garlic. Remove from heat and add parsley. Drizzle mixture over popcorn. Sprinkle cheese on top.

PEANUT BUTTER MAPLE-POPPED CORN

1 tablespoons peanut butter   2 teaspoons maple syrup
1 teaspoon butter   1 large bowl popped corn

In small saucepan, melt peanut butter and butter. Remove from heat. Stir in maple syrup. Drizzle over corn. Mix well.

TORTILLA CHIPS

12 natural corn tortillas   ½ tsp. garlic powder
1 tablespoons raw butter   ½ tsp. chili powder

Preheat over to 275°. Cut tortillas into quarters and lay on large cookie sheet. Combine remaining ingredients and brush over top of tortillas. Bake 20 to 30 minutes, until crisp. **Makes 48 chips**.

MINI PIZZAS

4 pieces of whole wheat pita bread
1 cup drained spinach, chopped
1 cup natural spaghetti sauce

2 cups grated raw Cheddar cheese
1 onion, chopped
1 green pepper, chopped

Lay pita bread on large cookie sheet. Spread spaghetti sauce evenly over bread. Add vegetables, then top with cheese. Bake at 350° for 30 minutes or until cheese starts to bubble. **Makes 4 mini pizzas**.

NACHO PIZZA

4 whole wheat flour tortillas
1 large onion, finely chopped
1 cup shredded Mozzarella cheese

1 (12 ounce) jar natural picante sauce
2 tomatoes, chopped
1 green pepper, finely chopped

Cut tortillas into quarters, making 16 wedges. Place vegetables evenly on wedges on 2 baking sheets. Spoon sauce over vegetables and top with cheese. Bake at 350° for 15 minutes or until cheese starts to brown. **Serves 10 to 12**.

CELERY NIBBLERS

8 large stalks celery
1 (16 ounce) can drained kidney beans
½ cup grated Cheddar cheese

⅛ teaspoon chili powder
Dash of salt

Mash beans with potato masher until beans are creamy. Add a couple drops of olive oil to make more creamy. Add cheese and chili powder. Mix in saucepan on low heat until cheese melts. Cool, then spread on celery stalks. Refrigerate in airtight container.

NOTES

Meals *of the* Mediterranean

Greece
Italy
Israel
Egypt
Turkey

10

Meals of the Mediterranean

In the fall of 1998, my husband, my son and I were privileged to travel the Mediterranean and observe and enjoy the dietary habits of several Mediterranean countries. These countries include Israel, Greece, Turkey, Egypt and Italy. We noticed some similarities of these countries in dietary habits. They eat a considerably more healthy diet than the average American. Olive Oil is their principal fat which usually goes hand in hand with their use of fresh garlic. The majority of their diet consists of fruits, vegetables, legumes, and grains. They have a very low consumption of red meat and an overall much smaller sweet tooth than we do in the United States.

I must tell you, out of the recipes I have shared with you from the mediterranean, mine and my husband's favorite is spanakopita (spinach pie from Greece). I make it at least every six to eight weeks. It freezes well.

TURKISH CHICKPEA, CHICKEN AND RICE SOUP

2 cans chick peas	4 cans chicken broth
½ cup brown rice	1 medium onion chopped
2 garlic cloves minced	2 tablespoon olive oil
1 teaspoon cinnamon ground	¼ teaspoon cumin (ground)

In large soup pot, combine peas, chicken broth and rice. Cook over low heat for 20 minutes. In small skillet, sauté onion and garlic in oil until soft but not browned. Stir in cinnamon and cumin. Cook for 5 of more minutes. Stir the onion mixture into the soup. Simmer for 5 minutes, then serve.

EGYPTIAN LENTIL SOUP

1 carrot, peeled and chopped	1 onion, chopped
2 to 3 ounces ground beef	2 tablespoons olive oil
1 teaspoon cumin (ground)	1½ cups lentils
8 cups water	1 cup spinach chopped

Check lentils for debris. Wash. In large soup pot, sauté onion, carrot, and beef until beef is browned. Stir in cumin, lentils, water and spinach. Cook until lentils are tender, about thirty minutes. Season to taste. Top with chopped onions if desired. **Serves 6 to 8**.

MEDITERRANEAN MEZE WITH PITA (FLATBREAD)

1 package whole wheat pita bread	4 tablespoons butter
1 tablespoon olive oil	½ teaspoon minced garlic
Dash of salt	

Open each piece of flatbread so you have two rounded pieces. Cut each piece in half. Melt butter and add remaining ingredients. Stir well. Using basting brush, spread butter mixture on each half circle. Place on cookie sheet. Broil in oven on low watching for a slightly brown color. Be careful not to burn bread. Serve hot with two or more spreads.

We had this one in Israel. A meze is a panoply of little dishes that are eaten informally.

SPREAD #1 — HUMMUS BI TAHINI

2 cans chickpeas

1 teaspoon salt

½ teaspoon cumin (ground)

½ cup tahini (sesame seeds ground into
butter; can be purchased pre-made.)

Juice of 2 lemons

1 tablespoon olive oil

½ teaspoon minced garlic

Place chickpeas in a food processor with about ¼ cup of water. Process until chickpeas are a coarse and grainy puree` (add more liquid if necessary). Combine chickpea puree in a bowl with tahini, olive oil, and salt. Add lemon juice and garlic; mix well.

SPREAD #2— TABBOULEH

¾ cup bulgar (cracked wheat)

½ cup fresh mint leaves, finely chopped

2 tomatoes, diced

1 lemon

2 cups fresh parley, finely chopped

1 bunch scallions, thinly sliced

½ cup olive oil

Soak bulgar in bowl with water for 30 minutes. When bulgar is nice and plump, drain, and squeeze out remaining water. In large bowl, combine bulgar and parsley, mint, scallions, and tomatoes. Squeeze slightly to release flavors. Squeeze lemon over mixture, then toss in olive oil.

SPREAD #3 — CACIK

1 long unwaxed cucumber

1 teaspoon white wine vinegar

1½ cups plain yogurt (non-fat)

Salt

2 cloves garlic chopped

2 tablespoons olive oil

1 tablespoon dried mint

Peel and slice cucumber. To draw more liquid out of the cucumber, place slices in a bowl with a little salt. Set aside for 15 minutes. In serving bowl mash garlic to a paste with ½ teaspoon salt. Stir in vinegar and oil. Add yogurt and mint. Rinse cucumbers and pat dry. Fold them into yogurt mixture.

TURKISH CARROT SALAD

5 to 6 carrots, peeled

½ teaspoon salt

4 teaspoons olive oil

¼ cup plain non-fat yogurt

4 teaspoons fresh lemon juice

2 cloves garlic, chopped and crushed

Boil pot of water. Put carrots in for 5 minutes. Remove from heat; drain. Cool down with cold water. When cooled, grate carrots. In mixing bowl crush garlic and salt together with the back of a spoon. Mix in yogurt, oil, and lemon juice. Pour this over carrots and mix thoroughly. **Serves 4 to 6**.

TURKISH RICE PUDDING

4 cups milk

1 cinnamon stick

Dash of salt

1 tablespoon rice flour

¾ cup fructose

Zest of 1 lemon

½ cup brown or basmati rice

2 cups water

1 tablespoon cornstarch

In a saucepan, heat milk almost to a boil. Add lemon zest and cinnamon stick. Keep heating milk for 30 more minutes, just below boiling. In another pan cook rice with 1½ cups of water until rice is tender. Add more water if needed. When rice is soft remove lemon zest and cinnamon stick from milk; pour milk into pan with rice. Simmer for 30 minutes. Combine rice flour. cornstarch, and ½ cup of water to make a smooth paste. Slowly add this to rice, stirring constantly, and cook for 10 minutes. Add fructose and continue cooking for 10 to 15 minutes, until pudding thickens. Garnish with ground cinnamon.

SPAGHETTI AND MEATBALLS

1 clove minced garlic	1 teaspoon oregano
3 tablespoons olive oil	1 teaspoon basil
1 (32 ounce) bottle natural	1 medium tomato chopped
spaghetti sauce	½ teaspoon thyme
2 large onions chopped	1 cup sliced mushrooms
1 cup cooked lentils	1 tablespoon barley miso
1 large green pepper chopped	1 tablespoon fresh chopped parsley

Sauté garlic and onions in oil. Add remaining ingredients except miso. Cover and simmer for 40 minutes. Take one cup of sauce: add miso and stir until smooth. Pour this back into the sauce and stir well. Simmer for 3 minutes on low.

Meatballs:

1 cup water	1 small onion minced
1 yard egg	½ teaspoon garlic powder
1 cup soy burger	1 tablespoon tamari sauce
½ cup whole wheat flour	1 tablespoon fresh chopped parsley

Mix together ingredients and form into ½ inch balls. Place in baking dish. Bake at 350° for 20 minutes. Fold meatballs into sauce. Serve over noodles. **Serves 6**.

Add more sauce if you prefer sauce not as thick.

ITALIAN CORNMEAL CAKE

1½ sticks butter

3 large eggs separated

1 teaspoon vanilla

½ cup yellow cornmeal

1 teaspoon baking powder

Dash of salt

1 cup fructose

½ cup blanched almonds. finely chopped

3 tablespoons orange juice

½ cup unbleached white flour

2 tablespoons arrowroot

Preheat oven to 350°. Lightly butter and flour one 9-inch round cake pan. In mixing bowl, cream butter; slowly add fructose. Add egg yolks one at a time; continue beating. Stir in almonds, vanilla, and orange juice. Add corn meal. Mix together flour, baking powder, and arrowroot; set aside.

In metal or glass bowl with clean beaters, beat egg whites until they peak. Fold in egg whites alternating with flour mixture, ending with egg whites. Pour in pan; bake 20 to 30 minutes, until cake springs back to touch.

GREEK GARLIC CABBAGE

2 small cabbages

1 clove garlic minced

Dash of salt

½ cup olive oil

Preheat oven to 400. Trim cabbage and cut into quarters. Remove center of central stem. Bring large pot of water with salt to a boil. Boil cabbage 5 to 7 minutes, until cabbage is softened. Combine garlic and oil in shallow dish. Drain cabbage and dip into oil. Coat each side. Place cabbage in baking dish and pour remaining oil over cabbage quarters. Cover with foil and bake for 5 to 10 minutes. **Serves 8¼ pieces**.

GREEK GARLIC SAUCE

1 bake potato, skin removed	1 cup walnuts, finely chopped
3 cloves garlic, minced	½ cup olive oil
¼ cup plain yogurt (non-fat)	1 teaspoon lemon juice

Crush garlic and ½ teaspoon salt until smooth. Add walnut and potato. Mash together until smooth. Stir in olive oil. ¼ cup a little at a time. Add yogurt; mix well. Add remaining oil. Stir in lemon juice. Salt and pepper to taste. Serve over vegetables or fish.

BRAISED SALMON

2 pounds Salmon or Roughy	1 teaspoon salt
(about 1 inch thick)	juice of ½ lemon
1 medium yellow onion, thinly sliced	¼ cup flour
2 bay leaves	3 tablespoons olive oil
1 clove garlic minced	½ teaspoon paprika

Preheat oven to 370°. Dip fish in flour, shaking off excess. Brown fish in 2 tablespoons of olive oil about 2 to 3 minutes on each side. Transfer to baking dish; lay flat. Mix together onion, garlic, bay leaf, and remaining olive oil. Pour in pan in which fish was cooked. Cook over low heat until onion is very soft, about 10 to 15 minutes. Remove bay leaves and stir in paprika and lemon juice. Pour this over fish. Bake for 20 to 25 minutes.

GREEK SPINACH PIE — SPANAKOPITA

We discovered spanakopita at a Greek meat market in Tarpon Springs. The pastry used in this recipe is phyllo. Phyllo is not the normal pastry that most of us are used to baking with, but once you learn how to use it, it's lots of fun. If your local grocery store does not carry this, I have found some store managers will order it if they have a manufacturer's name.

½ box phyllo	Olive oil
2 package frozen spinach, squeezed to remove water	1 package Feta cheese
	2 large onions, chopped
1 bunch fresh dill	

Preheat oven to 350° Saute onions in 1 tablespoon of oil. Add spinach, dill, and Feta. Mix well and cook on a low heat for 5 minutes. Lay phyllo on counter. (Keep moist with damp cloth.) In a large casserole dish brush a thin layer of oil on bottom of dish. Take one layer of phyllo, the size of your dish, and lay in bottom of dish. Brush with light amount of oil. Repeat with 6 to 7 layers of phyllo. Spread spinach mixture over phyllo. Add 7 to 8 layers of phyllo, alternating with oil. Baste top layer of phyllo with oil. With sharp knife, cut into 2 inch squares. Bake at 350° for 35 to 40 minutes or until top becomes a light tan color. **Serves 4 to 6**.

ANTI-PASTO SALAD

1 romaine lettuce (large head),
  torn into small pieces
1 cucumber, cut down the center, then
  ¼ inch slices in half-moon shape,
  then cut slices in half
1 package Provolone cheese, cut
  into ¼ cubes
⅛ cup vinegar

1 can kidney beans
1 can garbanzo beans
2 tomatoes, sliced, then cut
  slices in halves
1 jar artichoke hearts, drained
¼ cup olive oil
⅛ teaspoon salt

Place all on a large oval or round tray (glass or plastic). This is a fun salad because it looks like a work of art when you are finished. Arrange torn lettuce evenly in the center of the tray. Place kidney beans around lettuce in a circle. Place cucumber half slices, touching one another, and the flat side touching the beans. Place tomato half slices around cucumber in the same way. Place garbanzo beans in a mound on top of the lettuce. Place cubed cheese on top of the garbanzo beans. Arrange the artichokes on the kidney beans about ½ inch apart. Mix oil, vinegar, and salt. Pour evenly over salad. **Serves 8 to 10**.

Healthy
Holidays

11

Healthy Holidays

Helpful Hints for Holiday Baking

- A pie crust will be more easily made and better if all the ingredients are cool.

- The lower crust should be placed in the pan so that it covers the surface smoothly. Be sure no air lurks beneath the surface, for it will push the crust out of shape in baking.

- Folding the top crust over the lower crust before crimping will keep the juices in the pie.

- In making custard type pies, bake at a high temperature for about ten minutes to prevent a soggy crust, then finish baking at a low temperature.

- Fill cake pans about two-thirds full and spread batter well into corners and to the sides, leaving a slight hollow in the center.

- The cake is done when it shrinks slightly from the sides of the pan or if it springs back when touched lightly with the finger.

- After a cake comes from the oven, it should be placed on a rack for about 5 minutes, then the sides should be loosened and the cake turned out on a rack to finish cooling.

- Cakes should not be frosted until thoroughly cool.

- Kneading the dough for a half minute after mixing improves the texture of baking powder biscuits.

- Cut drinking straws into short lengths and insert through slits in pie crusts to prevent juice from running over in the oven and to permit steam to escape.

- If your juice from your apple pie runs over in the oven, shake some salt on it, which causes the juice to burn to a crisp so it can be removed.

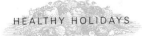

Enjoying Healthy Holidays

Everyone should enjoy the holidays and the special "goodies" that are so abundant that time of year. Just remember that moderation is the key and, again I repeat, it's not what you eat between Christmas and New Year's that can hurt you, but it's what you eat between New Year's and Christmas that can do the damage.

I have taken the popular "traditional" holiday dishes and changed them around to make them more nutritious but still tasting good. If you are going to be serving these to friend and family that are not health conscious, you might want to add a little salt to the main dishes and a little extra honey to the desserts. This will make it easier to win your company over to a more healthy way of eating.

If you have a traditional family holiday recipe that is served at every holiday but you no longer want to use the same ingredients, try this:

1. Decide which ingredients you want to substitute.

2. Choose the substitute.

3. Decide if there are any ingredients you would like to eliminate without drastically changing the taste.

Here's our favorite cookie recipe that's great to have around during the holiday season.

GRANDMA BROER'S NO SUGAR COOKIES

½ cup pears or apples chopped   1 cup whole wheat flour

½ cup chopped dates   1 cup rolled oats

1 cup pear (or apple juice)   1 teaspoon Baking soda

¼ cup butter   1 tablespoon Vanilla

2 eggs, well beaten

Boil first 4 ingredients for 3 minutes on low heat. Add butter and let cool. Add remaining ingredients and mix well. Refrigerate over night. Drop by spoonfuls on greased cookie sheet. Bake at 350° for 10 to 12 minutes. Store in refrigerator. (I usually double this recipe.)

Holiday Hospitality

Buffet Setting

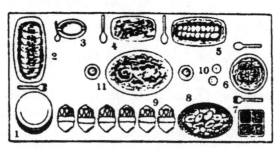

A buffet makes it easy to serve a large group in a small dining area. This setting can be used for any meal by just placing the food in the order of your menu, plates first and eating utensils last.

1. Plates

2. Main dish

3. Gravy boat on liner plate

4. Vegetables dish

5. Other side dish

6. Salad Bowl

7. Relish tray

8. Basket of rolls

9. Napkins with knives, fork, and spoons

10. Salt and Pepper

11. Centerpiece and candles

Luncheon

A luncheon can be great fun no matter what size the crowd. An optional fruit or soup first course could be followed by:

- Hot casserole or omelet, bread and a light dessert.
- Cold combination salad, bread, and a rich dessert.
- Small salad, hot main dish, and dessert.

Luncheon place setting:

1. Bread and butter plate and knife

2. Water glass

3. Optional drinking glass

4. Napkin

5. Luncheon fork

6. Dessert fork

7. First course bowl and liner plate

8. Luncheon plate

9. Knife

10. Teaspoon

11. Soup spoon

Dinner

You don't have to wait for a special occasion to have a formal dinner party. Sunday dinners with family and friends is a wonderful reason to celebrate by serving a formal dinner and it will almost guarantee help with the extra dishes!

1. Salad plate

2. Water glass

3. Optional drink glass

4. Napkin

5. Salad fork

6. Dinner fork

7. Dessert fork

8. First course bowl and liner plate

9. Dinner plate

10. Dinner knife

11. Teaspoon

12. Soup spoon

Napkin Folding

I always thought it was so nice to have folded napkins when eating out. Try these for your next fellowship dinner or party.

Butterfly

- Form a triangle from an open napkin. Fold the right corner to the center.
- Take the left corner up to center, making a diamond. Keeping the loose points at the top, turn the napkin over, then fold upward to form a triangle.
- Tuck the left corner into the right. Stand up napkin; turn it around, then turn the petals down; it's now a butterfly.

Artichoke

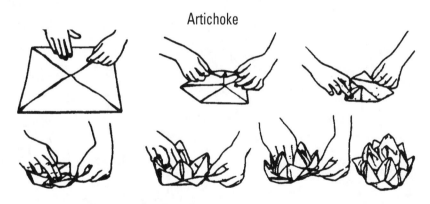

- Place all 4 points to the center of an opened napkin.
- Fold the 4 points to the center of the napkin once more.
- Repeat a third time; turn napkin over and fold points to the center once more.
- Holding finger firmly at center, unfold 1 petal first from underneath each corner.
- Pull out 4 more from between petals. Then pull out the next 4 under the petals.
- The artichoke now has 4 points.

Silver Buffet

- Fold the napkin over twice to form a square. Hold the square in a diamond shape.
- Take the top 2 flaps and roll them halfway down the napkin.
- Fold under the right and left points at the sides. There is now a pocket into which you can place the knife, fork, and spoon.

Quantities to Serve 100 People

Soup . . . . 5 Gallons

Meatloaf . . . . 24 Pounds

Beef . . . . 40 Pounds

Ground Chuck (hamburgers) . . . . 30-36 Pounds

Turkey Hot dogs . . . . 25 Pounds

Chicken . . . . 40 Pounds

Potatoes . . . . 35 Pounds

Scalloped Potatoes . . . . 5 Pounds

Vegetables . . . . 4 (no. 10) cans or 26 Pounds

Baked Beans . . . . 5 Pounds

Beets . . . . 30 Pounds

Cauliflower . . . . 18 Pounds

Cabbage for Slaw . . . . 20 Pounds

Carrots . . . . 33 Pounds

Bread . . . . 10 Loaves

Rolls 200

Butter . . . . 3 Pounds

Potato Salad . . . . 12 Quarts

Fruit Salad . . . . 20 Quarts

Vegetable Salad . . . . 20 Quarts

Lettuce . . . . 20 Heads

Salad Dressing . . . . 3 Quarts

Pies 18

Cakes 8

Ice Cream . . . . 4 Gallons

Cheese . . . . 3 Pounds

Olives . . . . 1¾ Pound

Pickles . . . . 2 Quarts

Nuts . . . . 3 Pounds (sorted)

To serve 50 people, divide by 2

To serve 25 people, divide by 4

Carving the Turkey

How to carve turkey

1. Remove leg; hold drumstick firmly, pulling gently away from body. Cut skin between leg and body. Press leg downward and cut from body. Separate drumstick and thigh; slice meat from each piece.

2. Cut into white meat parallel to wing, making a cut deep into the breast to the body frame, as close to the wing as possible.

3. Slice white meat. Beginning at front starting halfway up breast, cut thin slices of white meat down the cut. Slices will fall away from turkey as cut. Continue until enough meat has been carved for first servings. Carve more as needed.

Helpful hints to the hostess

- A large roast can be carved more easily after it stands for about 30 minutes.

- When garnishing, don't be over-generous; leave space for the work to be done.

- Servings cool quickly so plates and platter must be heated.

- An inexperienced carver will appreciate a hostess who keeps the guest's attention diverted from his carving.

- Convention doesn't forbid your standing up to carve, so, if it's easier, stand up.

- The bones get in your way if you don't know where to expect them; a little investigation tells you just where they are.

- Carving is unduly complicated by a dull knife.

- And remember the first rule of carving…"cut across the grain." If you cut with the grain, long meat fibers give a stringy texture to the slice. Steaks are the exception.

PECAN CORN BREAD DRESSING

1 batch Sweet Cornbread (see
   recipe in chapter 4)

10 slices whole wheat bread

6 yard eggs, hard boiled and chopped

2 teaspoons sea salt (optional)

1 large stalk celery, chopped

1 large apple, chopped

½ cup chopped pecans

2 tablespoons olive oil

1 tablespoon poultry seasoning

1 tablespoon parsley

2 – 3 cans Health Valley
   chicken broth

2 large onions chopped

In a large skillet, sauté onions in oil. Add celery, In large bowl, crumble corn bread into fine crumbs. Add broth and mix well. Add remaining ingredients. Mix well and spread in large baking dish. Bake at 350° to 30 minutes or until top starts to brown. **Serves 10 to 12**.

QUICK GRAVY

When you need a quick gravy base that is always low in fat, try Haines dark gravy mix. It mixes well with the juice from the turkey.

BAKED CORNISH HENS AND WILD RICE

(A great alternative if you are tired of turkey for Thanksgiving.)

2 to 4 cornish hens cleaned

3 tablespoons butter

1 tablespoon worcestershire sauce

1 tablespoon tamari sauce

1 teaspoon garlic powder

1 tablespoon honey

¼ cup water

⅛ teaspoon sea salt

Place hens in a shallow baking dish. Pour water in bottom of dish. Melt butter in bowl and stir in remaining ingredients. Baste hens with butter mixture. Bake at 350° for 1½ hours, basting twice. Uncover and bake for another 30 minutes. If hens are not completely done on the inside, cover and cook for another 30 to 45 minutes. Use juice in the bottom of baking dish to put on rice (Wild Rice recipe follows).

WILD RICE

3½ cups chicken broth

1½ cups brown rice

¼ cup wild rice

½ tablespoon garlic powder

1 tablespoon worcestershire sauce

1 tablespoon tamari sauce

½ teaspoon sea salt

Place all ingredients in a 3 quart pot. Bring to a boil. Cover and simmer for 50 to 60 minutes. Serve with hens. For great vegetable side dishes to go along with your Christmas or Thanksgiving dinner, turn to chapter seven.

Holiday Goodies

When baking for the Christmas holidays, I always seem to come across a recipe that uses red or green food coloring. Since I will not use artificial dyes in my baking, I found some excellent natural food colorings.

For red coloring: Beet powder. If you can't find it in bulk, buy beet capsules and just open up the capsules.

For green coloring: Use liquid chlorophyll (be careful it stains).

SWEET POTATO MEDLEY

4 large sweet potatoes, washed and sliced into ½ inch slices	¼ cup butter, melted
	¼ cup maple syrup
2 apples, washed, cored, and cubed	1 teaspoon vanilla
½ cup shelled walnuts	1 tablespoon ground cinnamon

In large casserole dish place sweet potatoes, apples, and walnuts; mix together. Mix together remaining ingredients and pour over sweet potatoes.Cover and bake at 350° for 30 to 45 minutes, until potatoes are soft in middle.

TOMMIE'S SPINACH BALLS

4 packages. frozen spinach, chopped and drained	1 large onion, finely chopped
	1 cup butter, melted
6 eggs, beaten	1 cup parmesan cheese
1 tablespoon garlic, minced	
4 cups seasoned whole wheat croutons	

Mix together all ingredients thoroughly. Chill 1 hour. Roll into balls. Place on ungreased cookie sheet. Bake at 350° for 15 minutes. Serve warm. **Makes about 100 balls**.

SWEET POTATO PIE

1 cup cooked sweet potatoes
¼ cup butter
½ cup sorghum
¼ cup brown rice syrup
1 tablespoon vanilla

1 teaspoon ground cinnamon
¼ teaspoon ground cloves
2 eggs, beaten
¼ cup whole wheat flour

Beat potato with electric mixer until smooth. Add remaining ingredients. Beat until smooth. Pour into 9 inch pie shell. Bake at 350° for 30 minutes.

SWEET POTATO CASSEROLE

3 cups sweet potatoes, cooked and
   mashed
⅛ cup fructose

1 teaspoon vanilla
⅓ cup butter
2 eggs

Mix all ingredients together. Place in a casserole dish and add topping.

Topping;

1 cup coconut
1 cup pecans chopped
⅛ cup fructose

⅓ cup butter melted
⅓ cup whole wheat flour

Mix well and spread over potatoes. Bake at 350° for 30 minutes.

PECAN PIE

4 yard eggs
½ cup sorghum
½ cup brown rice syrup

2 tablespoons butter
1½ cups pecan halves

Beat eggs. Add sweeteners and butter, then add pecans. Pour into 9 inch whole wheat pie shell. Bake at 375° for 45 minutes.

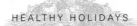

CASHEW PIE CRUST

1 cup cashews

2 to 4 tablespoons water

¾ cup oat flour

½ cup water

½ teaspoon salt

¾ cup barley flour

Make cashew butter by blending cashews and water until smooth. Cut cashew butter into both oat and barley flour and salt. Add 2 tablespoons of water and form into a ball. Roll in between two pieces of wax paper. Remove wax paper and place dough over pan. Form your favorite edging. If pre-baked pie crust, prick the bottom and bake at 350° for 10 minutes.

CAROB MINT BROWNIES

1 cup whole wheat pastry flour

1 teaspoon baking powder

½ cup softened butter

½ cup carob powder

2 yard eggs

1 cup chopped pecans

1 teaspoon vanilla

1½ teaspoons peppermint extract

1 cup fructose

In large bowl combine all dry ingredients and mix well. In blender, mix butter and eggs until creamy. Add extract and mix well. Pour in bowl with dry ingredients. Add ¾ cup chopped pecans and mix. Pour into buttered 8-by-11-inch glass baking dish. Sprinkle remaining nuts on top. Bake at 350° in preheated oven for 30 minutes for chewy brownies. Brownies will be easier to cut after they are completely cooled. **Makes 20 to 24 brownies**.

LEMON POPPY SEED MUFFINS

¾ cup honey

¼ cup butter

1 teaspoon grated lemon peel

2 eggs

2 cup pastry wheat flour

2 teaspoons baking powder

¼ teaspoon nutmeg

¾ cup milk

6 tablespoons poppy seeds

Cream butter, honey and orange peel; add eggs. Beat well. Combine flour, baking powder, and nutmeg; add milk until smooth. Fold in poppy seeds. Spoon batter into muffin tins, about ¾ full. Bake at 400° for 20 minutes.

QUICK PUMPKIN PIE CAKE

Bottom:

1 box yellow cake mix (reserve 1 cup; Simple Organics brand)

1 stick melted butter

1 egg beaten

Mix together until completely moistened. Press in bottom of greased and floured 9-by-13-inch dish.

Filling:

1 large (1 pound 3 ounce) can pumpkin

¼ cup fructose

1 tablespoon cinnamon

3 eggs

⅔ cup milk

In large bowl, beat with electric mixer and spread over cake mix.

Topping:

1 cup reserved cake mix

½ cup chopped pecans

¼ cup fructose

½ cup softened butter

Mix together and crumble over filling in cake dish. Bake at 350° for 45 to 50 minutes. Cool on cooling rack. Cut into squares.

PUMPKIN MAPLE CHEESE CAKE

1 ¼ cups whole wheat graham
   cracker crumbs
¼ cup melted butter
1 (16 ounce) pumpkin
¾ cup maple syrup

1 teaspoon ground nutmeg
¼ cup fructose
3 (8 ounce) package. cream cheese
3 eggs
1½ teaspoons ground cinnamon

Preheat oven to 300°. Combine cracker crumbs, fructose, and butter. Mix well and press firmly in bottom of 9-inch springform pan. Beat cream cheese until fluffy. Add pumpkin, eggs, ¼ cup maple syrup, cinnamon, and nutmeg. Mix until smooth. Pour into prepared pan. Bake 1 hour and 15 minutes or until sides spring back when lightly touched. Center will be slightly soft. Cool, then chill.

Walnut Maple Glaze:

2 tablespoons water
4 teaspoons cornstarch
2 tablespoons butter

Remaining maple syrup
½ cup chopped walnuts

Combine water and cornstarch. In small saucepan, melt butter. Add remaining maple syrup and cornstarch mixture. Cool until it thickens. Add ½ cup chopped walnuts. Spoon over cheesecake.

Awesome Carrot Cake

2 cups unbleached white flour
½ teaspoon salt
3 large eggs
¾ cup butter
3 teaspoons vanilla extract
1 (8 ounce) can crushed pineapple,
    drained
1 ripe banana mashed

2 teaspoons baking soda
3 teaspoons ground cinnamon
1½ cups fructose
¾ cup buttermilk
2 cup grated carrots
½ cup shredded coconut
1 cup pecans or walnuts, chopped

Line 3 round cake pans with wax paper (cut in circle to fit bottom). Lightly grease and flour wax paper. Set aside. Stir together first 4 ingredients. Beat eggs and next 4 ingredients until smooth with electric mixer. Add flour mixture at low speed until blended. Fold in next 4 ingredients. Pour into cake pan. Bake at 350° for 20 to 30 minutes or until toothpick inserted comes out clean. Cool on wire racks. Be sure cakes are completely cool before icing cake.

Cream Cheese Frosting:

2 (8 ounce) packages Cream cheese
    (or reduced fat cream cheese)
2 teaspoons vanilla

1 cup fructose
½ cup honey

Beat cheese until smooth. Add fructose and vanilla. Beat until thoroughly mixed.

CRUNCHY PECAN ORANGE CAKE

1 cup chopped pecans
¾ cup dried whole wheat bread crumbs

⅛ cup fructose
¼ cup water

Mix together all ingredients and press into an 8-by-11-inch glass buttered baking dish.

CAKE

¾ cup butter
¾ cup fructose
3 yard eggs
⅓ cup milk
1 tablespoon vanilla

1 teaspoon orange extract
3 cups whole wheat pastry flour
2 teaspoons baking powder
1 tablespoon grated orange peel

Cream together butter and fructose, then add eggs, then milk. Combine remaining ingredients and beat until smooth. Pour batter over bottom layer. Bake 45 minutes at 350°. Cool 15 minutes. Place bottom layer facing up. Slowly pour glaze over cake.

Glaze:

3 tablespoons orange juice
½ cup dry milk

¼ cup honey

Mix together all ingredients until creamy.

GINGERBREAD CAKE

½ cup maple syrup

½ cup molasses

½ cup vanilla low-fat yogurt

1 cup unbleached flour

1 tsp, ground cinnamon

½ teaspoon ground nutmeg

½ cup butter

2 eggs

1 cup whole wheat flour

1 teaspoon baking soda

1½? teaspoon ground ginger

Preheat oven to 350°. In large bowl beat together first 3 ingredients. Separate eggs. Set aside whites and beat yolks and yogurt into syrup mixture. Beat until smooth. Combine remaining ingredients in another large bowl. Mix well. Stir in egg mixture until blended. In separate bowl beat egg whites until they peak. Fold into batter. Pour into oiled and floured 9-inch pan. Bake for 25 to 35 minutes or until inserted toothpick comes out clean.

CAROB MACAROON MUFFINS

2 cups whole wheat pastry flour

½ cup fructose

3 tablespoons carob powder

1 tablespoon baking powder

6 tablespoons butter

1 yard egg

1 teaspoon vanilla

In large bowl, mix all dry ingredients. In blender combine fructose and eggs until creamy. Add butter and vanilla. Add this to dry ingredients, mixing well. Fill paper lined muffin tins ⅓ full. Add two teaspoons of filling to each muffin and top with remaining muffin mix. Bake at 400° for 20 minutes.

Filling:

4 tablespoons non-fat dry milk

1 cup unsweetened shredded
   coconut

1 tablespoon water

1 tablespoon vanilla

¼ teaspoon almond extract

Mix together all ingredients.

HOT CHRISTMAS CIDER

2 quarts unfiltered apple juice

½ qt. water (if too sweet, add
 more water)

2 cinnamon sticks, broken into pieces

½ teaspoon whole allspice

10 whole cloves

5 orange slices

Take spices and put in cheesecloth or sterilized handkerchief cut 6-by-6-inches. Tie together making a small bag. Pour juice and water into a 4½ quart pot. Add spice bag and 2 large orange slices. Bring to a boil, then simmer for 20 minutes. Pour into punch bowl and lay remaining orange slices on top. For a large number of guests, keep the pot on the stove on simmer and keep adding water and juice with the spice bag. This punch reminds me of Christmas. While it is simmering on the stove, the aroma fills the house with the smell of cinnamon and apples. I love using this for our Christmas open house. The bag of spices can be placed in an airtight container and placed in the freezer until you are ready to use it again.

EGGNOG

8 yard eggs

½ cup honey

Dash of ground nutmeg

4½ cups goat's milk (or skim milk)

2 teaspoon vanilla

In blender, whip eggs until they are creamy. On low speed add the sweeteners, vanilla, and 2 cups of milk, then mix well. Pour this into large pitcher and mix with remaining milk. Serve with a dash of nutmeg. **Makes 8 serving**.

Holiday Leftovers

When the friends and relatives have all gone home and it is time to make the next family meal, what do you do with the leftover turkey and dressing? Try some of these ideas for leftovers.

TURKEY CACCIATORE

2 to 3 cups leftover turkey

2 cloves minced garlic or 1 teaspoon
  garlic powder

2 tablespoons olive oil

2 medium tomatoes, finely chopped

1 large onion chopped

1 medium green pepper, chopped

1 teaspoon basil

½ teaspoon rosemary

1½ to 2 cups tomato sauce or
  meatless spaghetti sauce

Saute onion and garlic in oil in skillet until onion is tender. Add turkey, green pepper, tomatoes, seasonings, and tomato sauce. Cover and simmer for 20 minutes. Serve over whole wheat or artichoke pasta or brown rice. **Serves 4-6**.

TURKEY RICE CASSEROLE

6 cups cooked brown rice

2 cups chopped broccoli

1 large onion chopped

1 tablespoon olive oil

1 package Hains (or other brand)
  dry onion soup mix

2 to 3 cups cut-up leftover turkey

1 teaspoon garlic powder

5 slices multi grain bread

4 tablespoons butter

1 teaspoon garlic powder

In large skillet, sauté onion in olive oil. Add broccoli; stir for 2 to 3 minutes, then add turkey. Prepare onion soup mix for sauce directions. Add garlic powder to sauce. In large bowl mix together rice, vegetables, and onion soup in skillet. Mix well. Pour into large casserole dish. Crumble bread into fine crumbs over casserole. Melt butter and stir in garlic. Dribble over bread crumbs. Bake at 350° for 30 minutes. **Serves 6**.

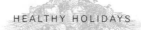

BROCCOLI AND DRESSING

4 cups leftover dressing   1 head broccoli spears

Spread dressing in an 8-by-8-inch baking dish. Make a very thin layer in center of dish and push dressing up to the sides. Cook broccoli until just barely tender, do not over cook. Lay broccoli spears on top of dressing. Pour cheese sauce over broccoli. Bake at 350° for 10 to 15 minutes.

Cheese sauce:

2 tablespoons butter   ½ cup milk

2 tablespoons rice flour or arrow root   1 cup grated Cheddar cheese

In saucepan melt butter. Stir in flour. Add milk. Stir until thickened. Stir for one minute longer. Stir in cheese until smooth and creamy. **Serves 6**.

TURKEY PILAF

2 cups leftover wild rice   ⅛ teaspoon basil

3 cups leftover turkey, chopped   1 cup cooked peas

½ cup chopped pecans   1 small onion chopped

1 tablespoon tamari sauce   ½ teaspoon salt (optional)

2 tablespoons mayonnaise

Mix all ingredients together. Scoop and serve on leaf lettuce.

TURKEY SALAD

2 cups leftover turkey, chopped   4 tablespoons mayonnaise

1 large onion, finely chopped   1 teaspoon sorghum

½ cup celery chopped   ½ teaspoon tarragon

1 cup carrot grated   ½ teaspoon salt (optional)

Mix all ingredients together. Chill and serve. **Serves 2 to 4**.

TURKEY SOUP

2 cans chicken broth

2 cups leftover turkey, chopped

1 package frozen spinach

1 carrot grated

1 small bag frozen peas

2 cups water

½ cup brown or basmati rice

1 large onion, chopped

2 stalks celery, chopped

In a large soup pot bring to boil chicken broth and rice. Simmer for 20 minutes. Add remaining ingredients and simmer for an additional 20 minutes. **Serves 6**.

BREAD PUDDING

4 slices sprouted grain bread, cubed

½ cup brown rice syrup

2 cups milk

1 teaspoon vanilla

4 eggs

1 teaspoon cinnamon

½ cup fructose

Beat together all ingredients except bread. Beat well. Add bread and pour into greased baking dish. Bake at 325° for 40 minutes. **Serves 6**.

Leftover Ideas

Cooked snap beans, lima beans, corn, peas, carrots, in:

Meat and vegetable pie	Stuffed peppers
Soup	Stuffed Tomatoes
Stew	Vegetables in cheese sauces

Cooked leafy vegetables, chopped in:

Creamed vegetables	Meat Patties
Soup	Omelet
Meatloaf	Souffles

Cooked or canned fruit in:

Fruit cup	Shortcake
Fruit sauces	Upside-down cake
Jellied fruit	Yeast breads
Quick breads	

Cooked meats, poultry, fish, in:

Casserole dishes	Salads
Hash	Sandwiches
Meat Patties	Stuffed Vegetables
Meat Pies	

Cooked wheat, oat, or corn cereals in:

Fried cereals	Sweet puddings
Meatloaf or patties	

Cooked rice, noodles, macaroni, spaghetti, in:

Casseroles	Timbales
Meat or cheese loaf	

Bread

Slices, for French toast	Fried chops
Dry crumbs, in:	Soft crumbs, in:
Brown Betty	Meatloaf
Croquettes	Stuffings

Cake or cookies, in:

Brown Betty	Toasted, with sweet topping, for
Icebox cake	dessert

Egg yolks, in:

Cakes	Pie filling
Cornstarch pudding	Salad dressing
Custard or sauce	Scrambled eggs

Egg whites, in:

Custard	Meringue
Fruit whip	Souffles

Hard-cooked egg or yolk, in:

Casserole dishes	Salads
Garnish	Sandwiches

Sour cream, in:

Cakes, cookies	Salad dressing
Dessert sauce	Sauce for vegetables
Pie filling	

Sour milk, in:

Cakes, cookies	Quick breads

Cooked potatoes, in:

Croquettes	Potatoes in cheese sauce
Fried or creamed potatoes	Stew or chowder
Meat pie crust	

Conclusion

21 Steps to Living a Happy Healthy Life

"Beloved, I wish above all things that thou mayest prosper and be in good health even as thy soul prospers.

— 3 John 2

All of us want to live a healthy, happy life, right? The desire to feel good and live well is a common ingredient in the recipe of human nature. But don't you know people who say they want a healthy life, but prove the exact opposite by their actions and lifestyle choices?

To live healthy today takes balance and discipline — traits that require too much work for most people. A balanced life is a goal to do what's best for your health, your family, etc., in a manner of not going in one drastic direction and realizing that "less can be more" or "variety is the key". A disciplined life is a life of doing what you know is right even when you don't want to do it. You decide you are working out today but your body says you are not. You decide that 2000-calorie desert tonight just isn't worth the extra hip rolls but your stomach says go ahead, it won't show up for 2 days anyhow.

Start implementing these 21 steps in your life. Don't try to do them all at once but try to add a few a week. You should start noticing a positive difference in your physical. mental, and spiritual life.

Step 1: Avoid the "Top Ten Foods Not to Eat"

1. **Pork**: high-fat luncheon meats, ham, pepperoni, hot dogs, bacon, and sausage meat.
2. **Shellfish**: oysters, scallops, clams, crabs, and lobster: the scavenger feeder on the bottom of the ocean. Also high levels of mercury.
3. **Aspartame**: Nutrasweet, Equal, See page 8, excitotoxins.
4. **Hydrogenated or partially hydrogenated oils**: see page 8–9.
5. **Junk food** (food with zero nutritional value): snack cakes, candy, cola's. My husband observed a "Twinkie" on display at a health fair. He asked, "What is a Twinkie doing at a health fair? The reply was a simple, "We're trying to determine its shelf life." My husband was amazed when he learned the Twinkie had been on display for the past fifteen years. Even God's bacteria is smart enough not to eat the Twinkie.

6. **Olestra, Olean** (the fake fat): One of most dangerous aspects of olestra is its ability to absorb (or steal) crucial nutrients an antioxidants bound to natural fats while it "passes through" the human digestive system.

   In addition to vitamin deficiency, olestra can cause diarrhea and rectal leakage.

7. **Caffeine**: If you are an avid coffee drinker and you want to know how you really feel, miss that cup of coffee one morning. If you are tired and feeling a head ache coming on, chances are you are addicted. Caffeine should be used as a tool not an addiction. Caffeine taps our emergency energy reserve system. When you need that extra energy it's totally gone because of the over stimulation of the adrenal system.

   My husband spoke with Mary Lou Retton about caffeine and she said that caffeine is a banned substance in Olympic competition.

   If you need to get up for a meeting or have a long trip ahead of you, caffeine can be very helpful. Caffeine is not addictive when used as a tool.

   According to the British medical journal, Lancet, just five cups of coffee a day will increase a man's risk of heart disease by 50 percent.

   Caffeine also contains a component called methylxanthine, which may actually increase a women's risk of fibroid-tumor formation in the breast tissue. Some researchers say this component may actually increase the risk of breast cancer in these same patients.

8. **High Fat Diary Products**: Sixty percent of the allergies afflicting people in the country are directly attributed to the consumption of dairy products.

   Cows' milk really isn't necessary for human health. We recommend certified raw goat's milk. Children up to the age of 2 need the high fat to ensure proper development. See " A Child's Diet".

9. **Chlorine in water**: Use a filter or be a filter. Chlorination of drinking water has been linked to bladder and rectal cancer. Chlorine destroys our cells just as it destroys the cells of other living organisms. Filter your water. Steam distillation and reverse osmosis methods can easily be done at home using a variety of units at reasonable prices.

10. **Alcohol**: Just 1 ounce of alcohol reduces the body's ability to burn fat by about one third. It also increases the risk of cancer of the liver and pancreas.

Step 2: Consume a High-Fiber Diet

- Lowers cholesterol levels
- Decreases risk of colon cancer
- Gives truth to the wise saying, "An apple a day keeps the doctor away."

Step 3: Eat Small Meals Throughout the Day

- Speeds up metabolism
- Helps to avoid that desire to over eat
- Puts less stress on the colon

Step 4: Drink Water

- Drink at least half your body weight in ounces per day of filtered water. Example: If you weigh 200 pounds divide by 2 = 100 ounces of water per day.

Step 5: Supplementation

- Take a high quality multi-vitamin daily, A.M. only
- Take B-complex daily (A.M. only, will give you energy)
- Take at least 2000 mg of Vitamin C daily
- Take calcium at night (has a calming effect)

Step 6: Essential Fats
(Omega 3 and Omega 6 Fats, Cod Liver Oil Caps, Flax Seed Oil)

- Helps rebuild and produce new cells.
- Helps with proper brain formation in infants and children.
- Helps elasticity of the skin.

Step 7: Trace Minerals

It is impossible to obtain all the necessary minerals we need from our food. The food is depleted because the soil has been depleted. A good trace mineral supplement is necessary several times a week.

Physical Steps (Lifestyle)

Step 8: Stress avoidance

- Stress depletes water soluble vitamins
- Causes premature aging
- Causes cellular breakdown (disease) and taps into energy stores

Don't over-react to situations, over extend your schedule, eat while watching TV, discuss stressful issues while eating; don't eliminate relaxation time.

Step 9: Sunshine

- Small amounts of sun exposure are good.
- Sunshine helps with the absorption of vitamin D

Step 10: Sleep

- Children grow while sleeping
- Sleep helps with cell rebuilding
- Sleep helps keep that youthful look
- Seven to eight hours of sleep a night is a good average for most people.

Step 11: Deep breathing

- Helps get oxygen to the blood
- Helps clean the lymphatic system
- Helps slow down aging

Twice a day at work, in your car, or somewhere you can be relaxed, breathe in for 10 counts, through your nose, hold for 20 counts, breath out of your mouth for 10 counts. Repeat this pattern five times.

Physical Fitness Steps

Step 12: Stretching

- Reduces muscle tension
- Increases range of motion
- Increases flexibility
- Spend 10-30 seconds in each stretch. Don't bounce.
- An excellent book for stretching in almost all sports would be *Stretching* by Bob Anderson.
- Along with stretching we recommend monthly or bi-monthly massage therapy. Find a well-trained massage therapist and you will never feel the same again. I especially need a massage after we have been on tour for weeks at a time. All the traveling makes me tense. Deep massage also helps the body eliminate lactic acid build-up from weight training.
- I also feel that a good preventative is to schedule in chiropractic alignment, especially if you have had any past back problems. I personally work out 5 days a week with weights and cardio and my son and I are black belts in karate, practicing several times a week. Because I am so active and have had a dislocated femur I visit my chiropractor once a week.

Step 13: Cardio

- Burns fat
- Gets the heart rate up
- Tones muscles
- Helps clean the lymphatic system
- Builds stamina

When someone mentioned cardio years ago, you automatically thought of running or aerobics. Now there is such a variety of cardio machines on the market today that almost everyone can find what suits them best. We use Precor elliptical gliders and they work well in the toning and firming without impact on the knees.

Step 14: Resistance Training

- Helps to reduce the loss of muscle tissue as you get older. On the average we lose seven percent of our lean muscle mass every ten years.

- Helps to maintain a stable metabolism. Every one pound of muscle you lose, you lower your own basal metabolic rate by fifty calories per day. So if you lose 10 pounds of muscle weight, you'll lower your own metabolism by 500 calories per day which means that you will have to eat five hundred calories less per day not to gain weight.

- Helps to maintain bone density

- Helps to maintain flexibility

- Helps to maintain a youthful outlook

- Helps to maintain good posture

- Helps to maintain circulation

- Helps to maintain a healthy heart and in doing so allows for greater blood flow to the extremities allowing individuals to reduce the risk of cancer, heart disease and diabetes. In addition, it helps individuals to maintain mental activity by allowing increased blood flow to the brain.

Step 15: Recreation

- Do something you enjoy

- Relaxation

- Take time to smell the roses and the daisies (or your favorite flower)

My husband at the age of 46, just now started playing golf. He is constantly being asked to play when he is out on his speaking tours but he never took the time to learn to and "just do it". One day he received a phone call from the owner of his publishing company to play in a celebrity golf tournament. Ted told him he had never played golf and didn't even have the right kind of shoes. His friend responded, " That's fine, we'll have fun and you will make us look really good," guess what — my husband plays now and to add, he enjoys playing.

I can't find anything more relaxing and unwinding than going to karate class with my son. The kicking, stretching, and punching helps me release all the tension from the day and also gives me some "fun time" with my son.

Mental and Spiritual Steps

Step 16: Attitude

Your attitude is everything. Webster defines attitude as: a feeling or emotion (mental position) toward a fact or state.

- Attitude is a choice, positive or negative
- What you think about, you bring about
- The Bible tells what we fear may come upon us
- A Proverb states: As a man thinketh in his heart, so is he.
- Attitude affects every part of your life: physical, mental, and spiritual.
- The words you speak can bring life of death.

There are four words we don't allow our children or ourselves to use in our home.

- **Hate** — just using that word gives you a negative feeling and causes your body to feel tense.
- **Stupid** — the word is not uplifting or edifying.
- **Can't** — Why tell yourself you can't do something? Your mind does not know the difference between what is real or not real. I can do all things through Christ who strengthens me. (Phil. 4:13)
- **Problem** — there is no such thing, we call them challenges.

Step 17: Forgiveness

Unforgiveness breeds bitterness and bitterness can breed disease. Having a bitter heart toward someone actually puts your body in a negative state. If you stay in this state for long periods of time or on a regular basis, your digestion will be drastically affected causing your body to not digest food properly. This is one of the reasons why some people have ulcers and irritable bowel syndrome and cancer.

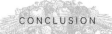

Step 18: Truthfulness

"Honesty is the best policy". You may ask, " how does being truthful have anything to do with your health?" Lying or untruthfulness affects the body, again, by putting the body in a negative state. When you are not truthful your body has a tendency to "tense up". I remember when I was a child and I lied about something I was supposed to do and did not do it. My stomach felt like it was tied up in a big knot and I worried about the situation all day. I was relieved when my father found out the truth and the spanking was over. The knot in my stomach left and I felt free.

Step 19: Generosity

Have you ever given something away and felt so good when you saw the reaction of the receiver? So many people are living their lives as takers; if they only knew what the secret of giving could do in their lives.

There are too many "tight wads" in the world today. Tight also means "tense". There is that word again. We all need to learn to free ourselves up from all the actions in our lives that tense us up.

If giving was not so important, God wouldn't have said in Acts 20:35," It is much better to give than to receive."

Step 20: Punctuality

Today we live in the busiest and fastest paced society that ever existed. Everyone has their "schedule" they must keep. In keeping these so-called schedules we "rush here and there," racing the clock, snapping at anyone or anything that gets in our way. This is not a very relaxed way of life.

Being punctual is an important character trait but not at the risk of your health. If you have a problem getting to your destination on time, I have some very technical advice for you —"leave earlier"!

We decided a long time ago that when you give yourself "a window," you totally reduce that anxiety that goes with a rushed schedule. Example: Let's say you need to meet someone for an appointment and you have a thirty minute drive to your destination. Instead of saying, I will meet you at 12:30; give yourself a window. Why not say, "I'll meet you between 12:30 and 1:00." You have given yourself a thirty minute window. That way if you get caught in traffic or delayed you will be relaxed more and not "stressed out".

Step 21: Love

Love is such an overused word but a word that says so much. Just say the word love and you get relaxed with a warm fuzzy feeling in your stomach. Now on the other hand, just say the opposite word, hate, and your body may tense even if it's the slightest bit. Spend your day trying to walk in love with others and you will be amazed how much energy you will have left at the end of the day. You will have less "stressed out" days. You will be healthier and more fun to be around.

We are three-dimensional beings;

Body — Physical

Mind — Mental

Spirit — Spiritual

To live each day to the fullest and walk in health and vitality, we need to work on three dimensions equally. That is what living a balanced life is all about. Here's to your health!

A Special Note About Our Nutritional Programs

If you want the very best products available — products that actually work — products that Ted, myself and my family use, read on.

Almost every vitamin, supplement, tape series, book or report that I have mentioned in this book can be ordered directly from our office. Just call 1-800-726-1834. You can also receive personal nutrition consultations over the phone by calling the same number. If you would like to become more involved in a total lifestyle change toward healthy living, consider these products:

Audio Tape Series

- The *Eat, Drink, and Be Healthy* Tape Program by Ted and Sharon Broer. An eight tape series that takes you through a systematic process of naturally lowering your cholesterol, high blood pressure, high sugar levels, along with information on Attention Deficit Disorder.

- *Forever Fit Tape Program* An eight tape series that helps you achieve increases in muscle mass, boost metabolism, and decrease body fat. It also goes into detail on vitamin mineral supplementation.

- *Living in Divine Health Tape Program* An eight tape series teaching optimal health and the secrets of scriptural nutrition.

Books:

- *Maximum Energy* by Ted Broer. Learn about the top ten foods never to eat in detail.

- *Train Up Your Children in the Way they Should Eat* by Sharon Broer. From preconception food choices to raising up healthy children

- *Maximum Solutions to A.D.D. and Autism* by Ted Broer. Natural treatments for A.D.D. and A.D.H.D

- *Maximum Fat Loss* by Ted Broer. Burn body fat and obtain lean muscles.

- *Maximum Memory* by Ted Broer. Foods that feed the brain and enhance memory. Three products that poison the brain.

Footnotes

1. WHO "Technical Report Series" 799 (1941): 40 (Evaluation of certain veterinary drug residues in food: 37th report of the joint FAO/WHO Expert committee on food additives.

2. National Research Council: *Toxicity Testing: Strategies to determine needs and priorities* (Washington D.C. National Academy Press, 1984).

3. Emilo Perez — Trallero, Mercedes, Urbieta, Carmen Lopategul, Carmen Zigorraga, and Isabel Aestaran, "Antibiotics in Veterinary Medicine and Public Health," *Lancet*, vol 342 November 27, 1993, p. 1371.

4. "EPA to study and insecticide for Links to Cancer," *New York Times*, October 24, 1993, pg. 21.

5. Winters, Ruth, M.S. "A Consumers Dictionary of Food Additives." Three River Press, NY 1978.

6. Food Products Development (December 1980): 36-40.

7. Kilham, Chris, *The Whole Food Bible*, Healing Arts Press, Rochester, Vermont, 1991.

Bibliography

Airola, Dr. Paavo. Are you confused? Health Plus Publishers, Pheonix. Az 1971.

Airola, Dr. Paavo. Every women's Book. Health Plus Publishers, Pheonix, Az. 1979.

Better Homes & Gardens New Cookbook. Meredith Press, Des Moines, IA. 1968

Boone, Vickie. Kaw Valley Dairy Goat Club Cookbook. Cookbook Publishers, Inc. Olathe, KS 1985.

Bragg, Paul. The Miracle of Fasting. Health Science, Santa Barbara, CA 1985.

Broer, Theodore A. D.Sc. Our declining health picture. NCS Ministries, Winter Haven, Fl 1985.

Broer, Theodore A. D. Sc. Fasting. NCS Ministries, Winter Haven, FL 1986.

Buist, Robert Ph.D. Food Chemical Sensitivity, Harper Collins Publishers Pty. Ltd., Sidney, Australia. 1986

Clymer, R.S. Prenatal Culture: Creating the Perfect Baby. The Philosophical Publishing Co., Quakertown, PA 1950

Crawford, M. "Essential Fatty Acids Requirements in Infancy." American Journal of Clinical Nutrition. 31, 1978.

Diamond, John M.D. Your Baby Doesn't Lie. Warner Books, New York, 1983.

Diamond, Stuart. "We Never Gave Our Water a Second Thought." Family Health, 1978.

Foman, Samuel J. Infant Nutrition, Second Edition, W.B. Sanders Co., Philadelphia, PA 1974.

Goldbeck, Nikki and David. The Supermarket Handbook. The New American Library, Inc. 1976.

Goodwin, R. Chemical Additives in Food. Churchill, London. 1967.

Holy Bible. The King James Version. Thomas Nelson Publishers, Nashville, TN 1984.

Holy Bible. The New International Version. Zondervan Bible Publishers, Grand Rapids, MI 1978.

Jenson, Bernard Ph. D. Food Healing for Man. Bernard Jenson Publishers, Escondidio, CA 1983.

Jenson, Bernard Ph. D. The Chemistry of an. Bernard Jenson Publishers, Escondidio, CA 1993.

Jenson, Bernard Ph.D. Colostrum: Life's First Food The White Gold Discovery. Bernard Jenson Publishers, Escondidio, CA 1993.

Josephine, Elmer A. God's Key to Health and Happiness, Power Books, NJ 1962.

Kilham, Chris. The Whole Food Bible. Healing Arts Press, Rochester, Vermont. 1977.

Mackenzie, David. Goat Husbandry, The Chaucer Press, Great Britain,1980.

Malstrom, Stan D., N.D. Own Your Own Body. Keats Publishing, Inc., New Canaan, CT. 1977.

Mendelsohn, Robert S. M.D. The Peoples Doctor, "Allergies: Part 1. "Vol. 3 Number 9. Evanton, IL.

Mendelsohn, Robert S. M.D. The Peoples Doctor,"Ear Infections"Vol. 5 Number 5, Evanton, IL.

National Academy of Research Biochemists. Volume 1 Number 5. Biloxi, MS May 1981.

Nave, Orville J. Nave's Topical Bible, Thomas Nelson Publishers, Nashville, TN. 1962.

Oski, Frank A., M.D. and John Bell. Don't Drink Your Milk, Wyden Books, 1977.

Price, Joseph M., M.D., Coronaries, Cholesterol and Chlorine. Jave Publications, Inc. NY 1969.

Shannon, Ira L. D.M.D. Brand Name Guide to Sugar, Nelson-Hall, Chicago, IL 1977.

Strong, James. The New Strong's Exhaustive Concordance of the Bible. Thomas Nelson, Inc., 1984.

Thomas, L."Hydrogenated Oils and Fats: The Presence of Chemically Modified Fatty Acids in Human Autopsy Tissue. " The American Journal of Clinical Nutrition 34., 1981.

William, Roger J. Nutrition Against Disease. "Pittman Publishing Corporation,1971.

Winters, Ruth. M.S. A Consumer's Dictionary of Food Additives. Three Rivers Press, New York, 1978.

Yiamouylannis, John Ph. D. Flouride, The Aging Factor. Health Action Press, Delaware, OH 1983.

Audio Cassette Teaching Programs by Dr. Ted and Sharon Broer

Eat, Drink, and Be Healthy Tape Program
By Dr. Ted and Sharon Broer

Our six week program to optimal Health and Energy!

Tape 1: The Top Ten Foods Never to Eat

Tape 2: Forever Slim (Do's and Don'ts of Weight Loss)

Tape 3: Winning Choices for Your Health

Tape 4: Double Your Energy, Double Your Output

Tape 5: Simplifying the Supermarket Safari

Tape 6: Foods That Heal

Tape 7: Food Choices: Facts and Myths

Tape 8: Answers to Our Most Frequently Asked Questions

Forever Fit 20, 30, 40, and Beyond Tape Series
By Dr. Ted Broer

Lose Weight* Feel Great* Fitness/Health Series. Our latest, up-to-date series on Health, Nutrition, Sports Medicine, and exercise!

Tape 1: Fat loss, Not Weight Loss — The Key to Looking Great! Hormones and How They Control the Body.

Tape 2: Exercise — Its Role in Burning Fat/Lean Muscle Mass – What Types & How Much

Tape 3: Trace Minerals, Vitamin Supplements, Fatty Acids/Joint Repair and Arthritis

Tape 4: Artificial Sweeteners/Chemicals and Foods in Our Environment to Avoid.

Tape 5: Chronic Fatigue Syndrome, Yeast Infection, Hypoglycemia. And Your Immune System

Tape 6: Constipation, the Colon, and Your Health

Tape 7: Fasting: The Physical and Spiritual Benefits

Tape 8: Water: Use a filter or Be a Filter/Why you absorb as Many Toxins in One Hot Shower as If You Had Drunk 8 Glasses of Contaminated Water.

Books by Dr. Ted and Sharon Broer

Maximum Energy
By Dr. Ted Broer

- The Top Ten Foods Never to Eat!
- The Top Ten Health Strategies for Maximum Energy
- Double your energy in 30 days with the right choices in this insightful book!

Train Up Your Children in the Way they Should Eat
By Sharon Broer

The ultimate children's program A must for every concerned parent

- Ensure the good health of your unborn baby.
- Nourish the infant and toddler so they can thrive.
- Protect and enhance the all-important immune systems of your children.
- Fuel active minds and bodies for complete physical and mental growth.
- Learn what your pediatrician won't tell you about your child's health.
- Stop serving the beverage that's more toxic than lead!
- No Ritalin
- No Ear Infection
- No Allergies

TO ORDER CALL 1-800-726-1834

Maximum Energy Cookbook
By Sharon Broer

A Health Guide to Survive! This book is an ideal gift for loved ones.
It includes:

- Back to basic recipes
- Infant, toddler, & children's diet
- Holiday Recipes
- Drinks, Shakes, and Coolers
- Fruit, vegetables, grains, and meat recipes
- Stress avoidance, exercise, water, goat's milk, and more…..

Maximum Fat Loss Book
By Dr. Ted Broer

You don't have a weight problem! It's much simpler than that.

- The Alarming Truth About Protein Diets.
- The 12 Step Program to Lose Body Fat, Not Muscle
- What Weight Loss Products You Should Never Use!
- 3 Easy Steps to Stop the Obese Child Epidemic
- The Key to Permanently Speeding Up Your Metabolism
- Discover 5 Secret Supplements that Melt Body Fat and Cellulite
- Why You Should Never Drink Diet Sodas

Maximum Fat Loss Workbook
By Dr. Ted Broer

A 12 week Program for Fat Loss!

- More Than a Commitment a — Desire
- A Workable Schedule and Plan
- Realistic Goals that Challenge and Rewards that Motivate
- Transporting Fat Out of Your Body
- Tying it all together

Maximum Memory Book
By Dr. Ted Broer

Would You Like to See a Significant Improvement in Your Memory and General Health in Only 30 Days, No Matter How You Currently Feel?

- The 10 Most Powerful Nutrients to Enhance Memory
- Alzheimer's Therapies That Really Work
- How to Boost Test Scores
- Stroke Prevention and Recovery
- Key Memory Building Exercises
- 4 Key Strategies for Stopping Senile Dementia
- 3 Products that Actually Poison the Brain
- "Smart" Foods and Herbs

Maximum Solutions for ADD (Learning Disabilities and Autism)
By Dr. Ted Broer

Don't let your child become a victim or a statistic!

- Top five foods never to feed a hyperactive child
- Truth about measles, immunization and autism
- Natural treatments for ADD, ADHD and autism

For More Information Call 1-800-726-1834

Other Audio Cassettes And Videos By Dr. Ted And Sharon Broer

Eat Drink and Be Healthy Exercise Videos
By Dr. Broer

A Scientific Approach To Athletic Conditioning And Proper Nutrition. It Includes:

- Lean Muscle Growth & Fat Loss In6 Weeks
- For Men And Women Of All Ages
- Three Tape Series For Men Or Women — 6 Total Tapes
- Lifetime Warranty On Videos

Understanding God's Dietary Principles Tape Series
By Dr. Ted Broer

This One Answers All The Biblical Nutrition Questions

Tape 1: How God's Dietary Principles Relate To Us

Tape 2: In Depth Scriptural Overview

Tape 3: How To Break The Dietary Curses Of Degenerative Disease

Hypoglycemia: A Sensible Approach Tape Series
By Dr. Ted Broer

Tape 1: Sugar & Controlling Hypoglycemia

Tape 2: Sugar And The American Sweet Tooth

Tape 3: What Has Happened To Our Health?

Nutrition and Your Healthy Heart Tape Series
By Dr. Broer

If You Have It, You Need This Series.

Tape 1: Preventing Heart Disease

Tape 2: Exercising The Smart Way

Tape 3: Stress And Your Health

Learn How To Keep This Critical Organ In Top Shape.

Natural Cooking for the Holidays Tape Series
By Sharon Broer

Tape 1: Using Meat Replacements and Grains

Tape 2: Holiday Meal Planning

Tape 3: Sugar Replacements and Holiday Desserts

For Those Who Ask; "Where Do I Start?"

Breaking the Dietary Curses of Cancer Tape Series
By Dr. Ted Broer

Tape 1: Cancer Prevention

Tape 2: The Benefits Of Fasting

Tape 3: Fiber And A Healthy Colon

Tape 4: God's Dietary Principles

Tape 5: Clean And Unclean Foods

The Nation's 2nd Largest Killer Can Be Prevented.

Helping Your Family Make Dietary Changes Tape Set
By Dr. Ted and Sharon Broer

Tape 1: Fiber And Food Preparation

Tape 2: Healthy Food Substitutes

Tape 3: Attitudes On Nutrition

This One Makes It Easy!

Preventing Arthritis and Osteoporosis Tape Series
By Dr. Ted Broer

Tape 1: Arthritis and Osteoporosis

Tape 2: The Importance of Calcium

Tape 3: Is Supplementation Necessary?

It's Easier to Prevent!

Train Up a Child In the Way He Should Eat Tapes
By Sharon Broer

Tape 1: Prenatal Nutrition

Tape 2: Infant And Toddler Nutrition

Tape 3: A Child's Diet

A Must For Those With Children.

Please Call 1-800-726-1834
For Current Prices And Specials

Index of Recipes

NOTES

This Cookbook is a

Perfect Gift

for Holidays,
Weddings, Anniversaries & Birthdays

To order extra copies as gifts for your friends,

Please use the order form on reverse side

of this page.

Order Form

Use the order form below for obtaining additional copies of this cookbook.

Mail to: Broer & Associates
100 Ariana Blvd.
Auburndale, FL 33823
(800) 726-1834

↓ Fill in Order Form Below — Cut Out and Mail ↓

Please Send More Information Concerning: ☐ Seminars   ☐ Meetings

Listing of Books & Tapes	Quantity	Price
_____	_____	_____
_____	_____	_____
_____	_____	_____
_____	_____	_____
_____	_____	_____
_____	_____	_____
_____	_____	_____
_____	_____	_____
_____	_____	_____
_____	_____	_____

Add $4 for postage and handling per book $ _____

TOTAL $ _____

Mail Order to:

Name_____

Address_____

City _____ State_____ Zip_____

Phone (_____) _____

Email Address _____

Please Call 1-800-726-1834 For Current Prices And Specials